To Tonya

God's blessings to
you and yours

David Ennis

Being the Dad
I Never Had

Dr. David R. Inniss

Being The Dad I Never Had

ISBN: 978-0-996-52250-2
Being the Dad I Never Had Softcover Edition 2015
Printed in the United States of America

For more information about special discounts for bulk purchases, please contact Innissense Publishing at 916.410.8817 or log onto our website at www.drinniss.com

Book design by Amy Green

*For my mother whose belief in me is limitless
and my sons Jalen & Nico who continue to bring
me joy like I have never known.   And to all of
my family and friends who loved me through
my imperfections and continuously remind me
that being my best is all that is needed.*

Table of Contents

"My biological father made me know that I would never do to them what he did to me. If there's breath in me and breath in them, they'll always be able to get to me. They'll never have to wonder where their father is or why he would leave them."

- Ray Upchurch, Producer, Daddy Hunger™

Foreword

A vivid memory that captures the heart of fatherhood for me is the image of my father coming through our front door to find four eager young boys running up and grabbing him by the arms. He would swing all four of us in a wide circle, as though he were an amusement ride personified. We would all yell out with glee, hoping that the thrill would continue endlessly. I can still recall the mixed aroma of us boys, the hydraulic oil on his work clothes, and his Old Spice cologne. This joyous moment of exhilaration encapsulates my father's strength and his active role in nurturing, affirming, and teaching us. He faithfully modeled what a father should be in the life of a child. His watchful eye, his encouraging smile, and his steadfast protection gave each of us an inherent understanding of what it means to be a good father.

Today, societal wisdom and media commentary offer little guidance as to what can be done to turn the tide of fatherlessness. The hopeless expectation seems to be that the cycle of fatherlessness and the resulting negative statistical data will only continue and increase. The negative outcomes of fatherlessness may readily be found in the form of disproportionate incarceration rates, juvenile crime, educational challenges, the war on drugs, and an inadequate foster-care system.

Rising above and beyond a sea of observations and analysis regarding fatherlessness comes the book *Being the Dad I Never Had*. The esteemed author, my dear friend David Inniss, suggests a bold approach in combating the spread of fatherlessness. He moves beyond hopelessness and repetitive cycles. Inniss uses his personal story as a backdrop, moving forward from victimization to victory and triumph. Few people can capture their past, their present, and their hope for future generations, as does this gifted educator. As a scholar, Inniss provides well-researched evaluation of the problems as well as thought-through, practical solutions. *Being the Dad I Never Had* gives the reader hope and models effective intervention using personal lessons applied with clear purpose.

Being the Dad I Never Had will equip fathers, fathers-to-be, mothers, children, educators, clergy, physicians, judicial advocates, and anyone that feels the effects of the physical and emotional absence of a father. The author gives a step-by-step approach to positive and healthy interaction with our children that can only be achieved by facing our fears, grieving our losses, and equipping ourselves with a vision for fatherhood that has not necessarily been modeled in our own lives.

This remarkable work stands in literary form as a true father's affirming presence and supporting arms, empowering its readers to move forward with renewed confidence that change and redemption are possible.

Parnell M. Lovelace, Jr., MSW, MPTh, D. Min

Prologue

Fathers are not necessary in the life of a child! They don't matter! As a matter of fact men aren't even needed. This is part of the story we often hear in popular culture. The men I studied over an 18 month timeframe say otherwise. They grew up without an emotionally present or physically available father. Yet, they offer a contrasting viewpoint. Their stories support the assertion that fathering and mothering are different with each having unique, necessary contributions to the development of children. The issue of fatherlessness is one that I have lived and studied for a lifetime. This book encapsulates the lessons I learned as I tried to become a great dad for my sons. Not perfect, but a present father focused on reshaping the legacy of manhood and fatherhood in my family tree.

With researchers committing thousands of hours to the study of gender psychology, feminine studies, masculinity studies, gender

1

dynamics and gender roles, the linkage between fatherhood and masculinity was found to be well represented throughout history. Starting with the pre-19th century era, fathers were the primary parent serving as the provider, moral guide, disciplinarian, companion and teacher for their families. Early 19th century urbanization and industrialization that was ushered in by the industrial revolution generated some changes in how fathers and fatherhood were perceived. Work demands outside the home shifted for men as a result.

The role of the father as the primary-parent seemingly took a back seat to his ability to work and provide financially for his family. Reduced time spent parenting altered perceptions of how involved fathers were within the family. To use a business analogy, fathers were considered the active family CEOs prior to industrialization, and were increasingly viewed as the disconnected chairman of the board for the family enterprise after it. The roles of primary planner, caregiver, nurturer and provider were somewhat eroded and replaced with that of arbiters of discipline. It is my speculation that it was during this era that the commonly heard phrase "Wait until your father gets home!" in response to sub-par behavior by a child originated. Increasing father-family separation and added pressure to be bread-winners created the perfect scenario for paternal apathy—physically and financially present fathers who are emotionally unavailable to their children.

The early industrialization era was deemed to be most responsible for the marginalization of fathers as parents. Post-industrial and post-world war periods were marked by globalization and an increased flow of information. With each decade, the general view of fatherhood and masculinity continued to evolve. The 1950s and 1960s saw the emergence of the "good family" man as families reunited after major wars. The 1970s brought the resurgence of the father as a dutiful bread-winner. In the late '70s, '80s and '90s, a social construction of masculinity as non-familial, transnational and business-focused took root. The resultant egocentrism and a declining sense of responsibility among men marked the beginning of a time when the fundamental value of fathers would be challenged.

By the early 1990s, family-based research disproportionately focused on the mother-child dynamic, reflecting social biases and the relative value placed on the roles of mothers and fathers. Increasing divorce rates and the growing frequency of mother-only families took root, confirming the emerging societal belief that fathers were peripheral to the family dynamic. A mid-1990s movement by a respected core of researchers sought to establish a link between father-absence and the moral decay of communities. The heightened scrutiny resulted in binary classifications of men as either good or bad, with more attention levied toward the bad examples of fathering. It was at this time that the term "dead-beat dads," referring to fathers who were negligent in financially supporting their children, grew in popularity.

A picture of a 21st century characterized by Haves and Have-nots—the fathered and the fatherless—was painted. The fathered group knew the daily presence and provision of a father and were considered to have the benefits of psychological, social, economic, educational and moral preparedness. The un-fathered group would not have these benefits. This idea of unequal access to various benefits positioned fatherlessness squarely as a potential issue of equity, which in turn caught the attention of social and political initiatives. An example was President William Clinton's issuance in 1995 of an executive memorandum emphasizing the importance of fatherhood programs, policies and research among government agencies.

With time, sophisticated studies offered support for the assertion that father-absence was related to sub-par educational performance, early childbearing and employment. The tide of the perceptions of fathers as irrelevant was changing. By the turn of the 21st century, with women participating fully in the workforce, the necessity of fathers and the essentialist view that they contributed in unique ways to the development of their children was slightly strengthened. Attentiveness to perceptions of fatherhood was highly encouraged while agitation for father-relevant social policies became more prevalent.

More than a century beyond industrialization—the event that kicked off a generally declining view of fathers—many still acknowledge fatherhood as one of the most important leadership roles in the world. In spite of the historical misrepresentation of fatherhood and anti-father rhetoric that infiltrated the discourse in many cultures, fatherhood is re-emerging as an important ingredient in identity formation and completion among children. Now, we can go to the park, sports fields, recital halls, dance studios, libraries, classrooms, gyms, PTA meetings, father-daughter dances, father-son retreats and parent teacher conferences and see committed fathers in action. Like me, many are coming from situations without their biological father as a model and are simply trying daily to lay it all on the line for their families—being the dad they never had.

Chapter 1
Scarred But Not Scared

I heard the footsteps stomping briskly down the hallway. My heart thumped in my chest, louder and louder with each sound of a foot crashing against the wooden floor. I sat on my bed in the farthest corner away from the door. I could hear the yelling of obscenities as the footsteps got closer. My bedroom door flew open and there he was…standing in the doorway. His eyes were bloodshot red and glazed over. His expression stern and every muscle in his body clenched. I had already assessed by the look in his eyes that he had probably had several shots of rum, maybe some gin and multiple beers.

"Who do you think you are?" His voice bellowed. I hunkered down, making myself as small as I possibly could. My knees to my chest, I sat and rocked forward and backward. His glare pierced my chest like a dagger as he continued to curse at me.

"Let me tell you something!" he screamed. "You see this? You see this? I am going to wipe your stomach out with this!"

I looked up as he raised his arm to reveal the 9 inch blade in his right hand, which formed a clenched fist around the handle. I recognized the knife. It was the most intimidating one from our kitchen but never before had I seen it other than as a tool for cooking. It had a brown wooden handle with black rivets, cleverly carved with grooves for a secure grip. The blade itself was silver, thin and long, about 1 inch at its base and closing to a sharp point.

I believed him! These were not empty words! The image of him hurting me with this knife was vivid. As he held the knife in his right hand above his head, my eyes were locked in on it. His image and all the anger he represented faded into the background as I focused on and recorded a mental picture of the knife—a picture that would haunt me for years to follow. I said nothing. I simply continued to rock, body compact as if not to expose my stomach to him. I would give him no opportunity to "wipe my stomach out."

He continued to hurl insults my way. I said nothing. I didn't whimper. I didn't cry. I didn't make eye contact. I wanted to do nothing to escalate this situation. Finally, he lowered his knife-wielding arm and walked away, his footsteps fading as he moved further away from my room. The emotional letdown, coupled with my fear got the better of me as I sobbed and shuddered at what had just transpired.

This was not a bad nightmare. This is my recollection of a terrible reality that occurred when I was six years old. The story that led to this episode is even more bizarre. My father came home after a day of heavy drinking with his friends at the local bar. The moment he entered the house, I knew that I needed to disappear. He stumbled to the dining room and sat at the table. Noticing my new electronic keyboard on the table, he pulled it toward him and attempted to play. Nothing. It needed new batteries and he got up to go get new batteries so he could replace them. In his drunkenness, he attempted to insert size D batteries in the slots that were made for AA size batteries. Often, when I reflected on this incident, this part made me giggle. Nevertheless, I watched as his frustration soared and in my own childlike innocence, I simply said "those batteries won't fit!"

Before, the words exited my mouth, I was met with a swift punch to the face. My instinct was to run. I had violated my own rule of becoming invisible if I detected that my father was not sober. He chased after me, pinned me on the couch with his knee to my back and unleashed a flurry of punches to the back of my head. I escaped again, and ran to my room and that is where he met me to share with me the plans he had for the 9 inch knife and his first-born son.

The fear, the intimidation, the feeling of insignificance this episode represented for me are still raw, even as I write about it almost 35 years later. The healing necessary to recover from such traumatic incidents is hard to come by and takes a lifetime to fully set in. It is against this backdrop that my insights on fatherhood were birthed. By the time the curtains were drawn for Act I of my boyhood, I had mastered self-taught survival skills to counteract the wrath of an alcoholic, physically abusive, emotionally unavailable father. It is from these experiences and several similar ones that I emerge—scarred but no longer scared, emotionally sore but ready to soar. It is from this life that I rise to have a candid conversation with you and share freely with you about how several scenarios like this, experienced and witnessed, have bolstered my commitment to becoming a great father and model for my sons—one who was different than the father I experienced.

Chapter 2
Our Conversation

One of my favorite things to do is to people watch. You can learn so much from simply being observant of the people around you. I would like you to try something. Take a walk in a park the next time weather permits. Take a seat on one of the benches. Relax and take in your surroundings. Feel the brush of the breeze against your face. Listen to the sounds around you. Maybe there are birds chirping. Maybe you can hear the squeal of children playing. Look around. What do you notice about the people you see? What can you read from their expressions and demeanor? Who are they with? Can you imagine their story?

If your experience is anything like mine, you will probably see a few seniors relaxing as they pause from their daily stroll. You will most likely notice a few moms chatting energetically about the joys and struggles of "mommying." It is probable that you will see a youthful couple doting on each other and enjoying the peaceful environment. There is a significant chance that you will also see at least one father, or maybe a few, fully engaged, playing on the play structure, throwing a ball or flying a kite with his little boy or girl, or pushing a stroller around the park, loaded with his toddler and the necessary elements of a park-trip survival kit.

The image of a dad at play in a public setting with his children is not as uncommon as it was a few decades ago. Like me, many fathers now embrace the idea of being highly involved in the early years of their children's lives. However, at various points throughout history, fathers were thought to be aloof, available primarily on weekends and only for a brief moment after work during weekdays. They were less associated with nurturing little ones and mostly thought of as disciplinarians in their household.

As expected, the perceptions held by many about the father role have changed significantly over time. Shifts in societal circumstances that affect the family unit, particularly men, have caused ripple-like changes in how people think fatherhood ought to be played out in society. Concurrently, the ever-changing cultural landscape of nations across the globe have caused many to rethink how manhood is lived out by today's men. With such changing social environments, history is replete with challenges to the role of men, particularly as fathers. Numerous questions have since emerged as many sought to understand effective male and/or masculine participation in the family unit.

The long history of shifting perceptions about manhood and changing demands on fatherhood brings us to today, this moment in which you and I are connected! I have written some thoughts and stories I know are rather important and you somehow have been sufficiently convinced to pick this book up to join me. To help with our connection, we are going to have to be able to speak a common language. I want to make sure we clearly understand each other in these limited moments we are spending together. So, let's clarify some terms.

I have mentioned the word masculinity several times and just for clarity, I think it would be smart to provide our working definition for this word. Masculinity has often been mixed up with descriptors of being male. Remember, being male is a physical descriptor that refers to the possession of male anatomy. Masculinity is different. The study of masculinity followed the outburst of attention paid to feminine studies. Both belong to a group of emerging disciplines that seek to explain gender-related issues.

There are three core aspects of masculinity with which we need to get on the same page. The first is that masculinity and gender in general is socially defined. It is impacted by the norms, culture and other social conditions that exist. The social construction of masculinity further implies two things. One, it is loosely defined and two, it is historically variable. In other words, the tenets that define masculinity are not concrete. Instead, descriptors are loosely assembled to provide a perspective of what it means to be a man. Also, perceptions about masculinity vary with time. What is considered masculine in one era may not be in another.

The second aspect of masculinity is that it is contextual in nature. This suggests that the definition of masculinity varies depending on the environment in which "being a man" is being considered. From country to country, city to city, urban to suburban settings, and ethnicity to ethnicity, masculinity may look slightly different in how it is manifested in day to day life. It aligns with the context within which it is being lived and observed.

Lastly, masculinity is plural. Plural? How can masculinity be plural? What are the implications of plural masculinities? Now this aspect of masculinity is often hard to grasp and that is why we should settle on what it means up front. This simply means that there may be more than one type of masculinity. Powerful research backed by numerous studies in the early 1980s introduced this idea that multiple masculinities existed. Some masculinities may be rooted in a man's ability to provide or protect. Others may rely on the display of "manly" mannerisms, constant proof of virility and a rejection of effeminate behaviors. Others still may embrace nurturing and caretaking—both of which are often viewed as feminine.

History has shown us that there is a strong linkage between widely held perceptions about masculinity and the beliefs held about fatherhood. Like masculinity, aspects of fatherhood are somewhat

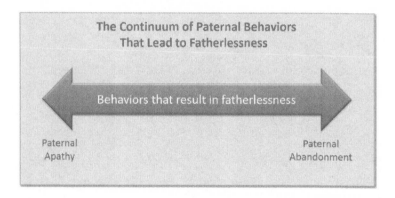

contextual, moving in and out of relevance depending on the period and circumstances in which it is being considered. As we discuss the relationship between masculinity and fatherhood, the conversation about what people believe about fatherlessness is inevitable.

Before you move forward on the exciting journey of this book, it is important the definition of the word fatherlessness is clarified. So what is fatherlessness? Too often we assume that fatherlessness pertains only to outright absence. Considering only the presence or absence of a father is actually quite limiting. Throughout this book, I define fatherlessness as a combination of physical and emotional distance between fathers and children that results from a continuum of paternal behaviors ranging from paternal apathy. Apathy primarily creates emotional distance between a father and his children while abandonment obviously physically separates them. Consequently, fatherlessness occurs when there is any combination of physical and emotional distance that is present in the father-child relationship.

Being The Dad I Never Had

Based on my life and exploration, fatherlessness is a human experience that has a highly personal impact on individuals regardless of race or socioeconomic class. From the mouths of men who have lived it, it ultimately affects one's ability to father. The personal impact sometimes gets lost in the shadows when the consequences of fatherlessness are described only in terms of numbers. Graduation rates, dropout rates, rates of propensity toward substance abuse, and incarceration rates are all numbers that are typically related to the pervasiveness of fatherlessness. While useful in many ways, these statistics do not lend credence to the actual experience of being fatherless as expresses by those who have lived it.

Throughout the remainder of this book, I speak specifically to the fatherless man who is looking for tools or techniques that could potentially level the proverbial "fathering playing field." There are several skills and approaches commonplace for those with a positive role model, to which fatherless men like myself were never exposed. I can attest from through my own personal journey and stories from others who share my experience that father-absence and/or paternal apathy have long lasting impacts that affected my own decision making well into my adulthood. I also speak to any father or aspiring father who is seeking guidance on certain aspects of being a dad. The recommendations, based on my life lessons thus far, are simply focused on developing universal competencies associated with positive fathering. I also speak to anyone who interacts with or who has experienced fatherlessness as I defined it.

CHAPTER 2 Our Conversation

In sharing such tools, I give you some insight into my story, my wounds, my pain, my healing, my shortcomings and my resilience. I share the life journey of a fatherless boy from a faraway island paradise who could not shake the impact of a dysfunctional father-son relationship despite his every effort to dismiss his experience. Although I did not list it as one of the lifelong lessons, I would encourage you to document and retell your story, even if it is just in the form of a personal journal. The act of sharing your story is extremely cathartic. I tell my story for your benefit so it may trigger your own thought process about how to tell yours and the benefits you may derive from telling it. I also share with you many of the insights that fatherless men I have met and conversed with over the years have shared with me. I have encountered and chatted with well over a thousand fatherless fathers so far and there are several commonalities in their experiences to which you will have access. I also attempt to capture how the experience of fatherlessness rears its ugly head in various situations that occur well into manhood. Knowledge of these long-term challenges is absolutely critical if you are to overcome or pre-empt them as you become that stellar dad you never had.

The absence of a father who taught and demonstrated what positive male citizenship looks like can leave a young father floundering and relying purely on intuition and gut feelings. While great intuition is an absolutely wonderful trait to have, it can lead to what I call trial-and-error fathering. Trial-and-error fathering works like this:

1. As a father, you are confronted with a situation for the first time with your son or daughter.

2. You reach back into your experience with your father but he was either absent, disconnected or unavailable.

3. With no reference point to draw on from your father-son experience, you resort to your intuition or best guess.

4. Your gut feeling leads you to an action rooted in your own experience—a natural response—that falls flat.

5. Oops…that didn't work…Let's try something else.

6. In going to an alternative plan, we may simply go with another gut feeling or choose to get some advice from someone we respect. Hopefully, those we choose to seek advice from can relate to our situation and understand our thought processes.

7. We go with the alternative and wait patiently to see if it worked or whether you have to consult your gut again.

While this may ultimately lead to the ideal solution, there are too many opportunities in the "error" segment of trial-and-error fathering to permanently wound your young ones. Surely, this is not desired. This quick handbook is by no means exhaustive but is applicable to anyone embarking on the wonderful journey of fatherhood. For those who share my experience of growing up without a positive father in your lives, fathering can be rather intimidating. Nevertheless, I uncovered a few mantras that worked for me, allowing me to love, nurture and care for my sons in a way I would never have imagined.

CHAPTER 2 Our Conversation

The seven life lessons that I believe can unlock a life of thriving after experiencing fatherlessness are as follows:

1. Establish the contract
2. Build resilient qualities
3. Be the best you, not a better him!
4. Teach! Teach! Teach!
5. Presence over perfection
6. Embrace the emotional man
7. Fill your fatherhood bag

Together, we will explore each of these in deeper detail and look at ways we can incorporate them into your everyday life practices. But first, let us dig deeper into the mindset of the fatherless man. Let us try to understand more about how many of us think, the commonalities in some of our approaches and the lifelong impact of father absence. I once heard a young man describe life as comprising a series of mental snapshots. He mentioned that his reel was dominated by the absence of his father, and he outlined his intention to make sure he would always be in the frame when his sons develop their mental snapshots. That is powerful imagery.

The journey toward coping effectively with the fatherless experience requires on-purpose action and resilience. There is no straight path to closure and restoration. Instead, there are several emotional cycles during which you will experience exploration of new aspects of yourself, pain and ultimately personal growth. While there may be many other approaches, I am confident the chapters that follow will resonate with you as you reflect on your past and project your future as a dad that you possibly never had.

Chapter 3
The Fatherless Experience

I woke up at age 30 and was inexplicably sad. As I contemplated the rush of feelings, I reflected on the potential sources of the emotional turmoil I was experiencing on this special day. The more I thought, the clearer it all became. What was the problem? Well, I had a physically abusive father. He was an alcoholic who repeatedly singled me out as a target of hateful rhetoric and wild threats. By age 7, I had been punched like a grown man, cursed at like a drinking buddy, and introduced to the knife that would be used "to wipe my stomach out." Those things became my "normal" and as a result, I developed some survival skills. I became an expert at quickly studying my father's eyes to determine his level of intoxication. My techniques became so effective that I could tell how many drinks he had had. In fact, my friends today marvel at this skill, as I am still able to do this pretty accurately today. With my perfectly calibrated assessment, I was able to determine rather quickly whether it was safe to remain visible throughout our small house or whether I should be cautious and hide away in my room.

At age 10, a violent break-up of my family took place after another evening of my father's binge drinking. This episode of threats and bullying was the straw that broke my family's back. Thankfully, my mother, my brother and I escaped from a situation that evening that could have ended up in tragedy. As a consequence, we were forced to move in with our extended family, in the house where my mother grew up. What I perceived as hatred from my father did not cease. Even though I was no longer around him, he continued to blatantly threaten to harm me until well into my teenage years. By then, I was sufficiently developed to protect myself and no longer felt threatened by his "hatefulness." Needless to say, this period impacted me heavily. I carried anger—a lot of it. I became the protector for my mother and a guide for my brother. I struggled to cope with the new living arrangements but acknowledged that it could have been worse.

Thoughts of this drama that unfolded in June 17, 1988 never left me. It would often be at the forefront of my thinking, triggered by some remotely related factor. Small, seemingly insignificant verbal or visual cues would take me right back to those moments. Simple experiences for me, carried more weight because they were loaded down with the baggage from my memories. As an example, I always find it quite interesting when a group of men who know little of each other's father-son experiences come together in a casual setting for simple banter and conversation.

Their conversations never start off being about exposure to paternal neglect. They are often lighthearted in the beginning, frontloaded with jokes and frivolity. I have witnessed many conversations like these and I can't help but think that they almost appear to be scripted. As the scenarios play out, I am always reminded of a set of actors, sitting around a large table, reading their parts of a script for an upcoming movie. The storyline is well known, with familiar characters and a predictable plot. Just like the typical action-revenge movie in which the main character is bullied in his early years, loses a loved one at the hands of "the bad guy" and then avenges his loss with lethal force, the conversations I refer to follow a tell-tale pattern.

For the most part, the conversations would take place like this. First, a situation takes center stage as the topic of discussion. It could be about a range of subjects—sports, politics, movies, music, women, local news, national news, travel, cultures, women, economics, race relations, careers, parenting, education or...yes, you guessed it...women. It appears that the topic of father absence, emotional or physical would find its way into these discussions. Inevitably, a critical moment in the discussion occurs when the topic inspires a statement about a father who was absent, demonstrated little emotional connection with his children, or was apathetic in his approach to fathering.

As an example, let's consider a conversation about sports. More specifically, imagine a conversation about America's pastime, football. Participants in the conversation have their favorite teams and favorite players. Who is the better player? Who deserves to be in the Hall of Fame? Who plays with heart? Who is the most "clutch" player? Which team will undoubtedly make it to the super bowl? As the conversation unfolds, discussion about individual athletes ensues. Given their "public figure" status, aspects of both their professional and personal lives are open game for analysis. Reasons surrounding the players' ability to make sound decisions or the rationale behind some wrong turns they make are proposed. Invariably, the guidance an athlete had or did not have throughout his life comes up.

For the majority of the numerous conversations of this type that I have witnessed, at this point, the room goes quiet for a few seconds as the seriousness of the issue takes hold. There is the obligatory shaking of the head, sighs and questions about why fathers have continued to "do this to their boys." Once this part of the conversation begins, there is often one individual—let's call him *The Initiator*—who becomes overwhelmed by the emotion of the conversation. It hits too close to home for him. The general chatter about a random athlete, actor, musician or politician and their experience with fatherlessness brings up some memories for him that are painful. He is reminded of his own experience.

CHAPTER 3 The Fatherless Experience

What takes place next is interesting. The *Initiator* ultimately falls on his sword and begins to share his story about childhood, pre-teen and adolescent years without the guidance and example of a present, caring and supportive father. It is an experience he shares with the athlete(s) that inspired the conversation in the first place. The *Initiator* is markedly shaken by his recollection and by now, the room is silent. Scanning the room, there is a range of responses to what is taking place. As The *Initiator's* story unfolds, there is head nodding, approving sighs and acknowledging words that emerge from others in the conversation. Let's call them the *Supporters.* There are blank stares off into the distance while some take individual trips down memory lane, reliving their own experiences—good or bad—with their dad. Some are clearly dreaming of "what it could have been like" if only they had more quality time with their fathers.

"I feel you, man!"

"I went through the same thing, brother!"

"That is crazy. I thought I was the only one that thought like that!"

"Are you serious? My father did the exact thing to me too!"

"Yes, my mother did it all!"

"I agree, I was always searching for that replacement!"

"I had to grow up too fast as well!"

"I had no clue how to treat the ladies either."

"I can see that!"

"I grew up very angry too!"

"I could never bring myself to trust men either!"

"Yes, our fathers did us just like their daddies did them."

"My mom did the best she could, but she couldn't teach me about being a man!"

"It's like I grew up with a big hole in my identity!"

The *Supporters* become engrossed in the conversation and they too supplement it by providing little vignettes that depict their exposure to a fatherless life. Some talk about good times when they believed their father made a difference to them. Others mention the moment when they realized there was an emotional or physical distance between them and their fathers. The common experiences create a bond in the room, further cemented with each story and each recalled scene.

Ultimately, another participant in the conversation emerges from the group. Let's call him *The Activator*. *The Activator* is forward looking. He absorbs all that he has heard. He listens to the damage and pain others have conveyed. He acknowledges what he heard as the potential impacts of growing up without a positive model of masculinity. As he listens, he ponders deeply on the desire to right what he perceives as a wrong. He wants the group to believe they can make a difference. After much thought, the *Activator* openly expresses a desire for change and makes powerful affirmations for those who shared this seemingly life-shaping experience. He encourages them to make a difference.

"We have to do things differently!"

"We have to do better!"

"We have to be there for our children!"

"We can't let them tell the same story!"

"How can we show up for our children?"

"We know better. So we have to do better!"

Were you ever in a conversation that flowed like this? If so, think about the last time. Who was the *Initiator*? What stood out to you about the *Initiator's* story? Do you remember some of the comments from the *Supporters*? What powerful declarations did the *Activator* make? What was your role in the conversation?

Personally, I have sat through numerous conversations that have followed this pattern. They are so effective at causing some powerful emotions to surface that I modeled this book after one of those conversations. Given the tens, hundreds or hopefully thousands of men and women who actually pick up this book and read it, we will become immersed in a virtual conversation. Worldwide, fatherless men like me and those close to them are engaged in a casual conversation that makes us think and sometimes share our experiences. While we may not be collocated in a room, our conversation is built on transparency and trust, and is one in which the voices of fatherless men are heard and respected.

With this book as a platform for our conversation, I have the enviable role of being the *Initiator*. You get to be a part of this conversation as the *Supporters*. As you read on, on many occasions we both will fall into being *Activators* as we identify ways in which those of us who have experienced fatherlessness in some form can thrive.

So, in typical Initiator fashion, I am moved to share with you my journey...my story...my experiences. It is a cyclic journey of pain, resolve and restoration. Punctuated with epiphanies and aha moments, this journey cemented my perceptions about my own boyhood and in many ways shaped the man I am today. My story outlines a path of a little boy filled with dreams and aspirations who goes through the emotional struggles of adolescence void of a paternal model. It takes you down the winding path of an early adulthood characterized by denial and continued feelings of rejection. Finally, it twists and turns into the years of maturing manhood in which I confronted my vulnerabilities and entered into the realm of fatherhood. Some parts of my experiences will resonate with you. As a matter of fact, I believe there will be some moments I describe with which you will really relate, and may have experienced yourself. Some aspects may not be applicable to you at all.

CHAPTER 3 The Fatherless Experience

My Story

I was born and raised in Barbados, a small island paradise
known for its unspoiled charm and unbridled sophistication. This
Eastern Caribbean isle has a rich history that began in the early 1600s
when it was colonized by the British. Life in this small country
demanded that communities pull together for collective benefit.
Almost everything followed a pattern of communal living and
collegiality in a village-like arrangement. Adults took great pride and
responsibility in rearing not only their own offspring but also all the
neighborhood children. Almost everyone placed significant value on
education—viewing it as a sure pathway out of poverty. The
importance of education was, and continues to be, a significant
influencer in a Barbadian upbringing.

If there is one word that aptly describes many of the
childhood memories I have, it would be "freedom." In my memory,
my boyhood adventures rival those of Mark Twain's fictional
characters Tom Sawyer and Huckleberry Finn. Summers as a little
boy were exciting. Large groups of my friends roamed all over our
neighborhood in search of the next adventure. I dare say that we lived
off the land. We sought out fruits that were in season and feasted on
them. Whether we sought the tree owners' permission first or simply
asked for forgiveness later, we perfected how we picked any fruit we
wanted. I distinctly remember mangos. Many of us could easily
assess the ripeness of a mango from a distance and had developed the
arm accuracy with the throw of a stone to knock the target mango,
and no others, from the tree.

Being The Dad I Never Had

I remember the creativity of my childhood friends. Necessity breeds ingenuity and we were not privileged with the latest gadgets. We made our own toys. Bats, balls, racquets! You name it…we made it! We made our own scooters and skateboards using ball-bearings. We became experts in kite-making. The kites we flew were expertly made using the branches of a coconut tree, stalks from sugar cane and plastic bags. Our model cars and toy trucks were beautiful works of art, assembled using blocks of wood and small cans. There was certainly no shortage of creativity at play during my childhood.

School at an early age was challenging and fun. Fortunately for me, my mother was a school teacher at the school I attended. I was known by all of her peers and they all took an interest in my academic success. I must say that I witnessed a cadre of teachers, my mother included, who dedicated their time and extreme efforts to ensure that children from all types of backgrounds had a shot at success via education. All of them went on to have long careers in excess of 40 years and in so doing, taught, uplifted, encouraged, motivated, and cared for thousands of children from various family situations.

This period of freedom and exploration in my early boyhood gave way to challenging but rewarding teen age years. I was a highly disciplined teenager. At the age of eleven, I was joyful at discovering my dream career. I became determined to live out my adulthood as a soldier—a light infantry officer to be more exact. My passion for this career path was powerful. I consumed so much literature about soldiering. I became a member of The Barbados Cadet Corps, a junior paramilitary organization that built confidence, discipline, respect and integrity in youth aged eleven to eighteen. All of this was done in the context of military training and by placing significant responsibility and trust in young men and women at a very early age. I owe so much of who I have become as a man to my experience in "the cadets."

With its rich traditions and long history, the cadet corps impacted the lives of several influential Barbadians. The lessons taught were life-long and helped me tremendously in handling many situations. The painstaking weekly preparation of a military uniform taught me about pride in appearance and deportment. The intensity of the military training showed me the value of meticulous preparation and the importance of working within the context of a team. The focus on leadership and merit-based advancement challenged me to set goals, work hard, rebound from failure, relish in success and appreciate the uniqueness in people. That experience was an inspirational start to my adulthood.

I experienced the entire gamut of emotions during my teenage years. I grieved the loss of my maternal grandmother. I awed at the strength and power of my mother—a single mother who really made life appear easy to my brother and me. I was joyful at discovering my purpose and career as a military officer. I was angry at the extent to which father absence impacted my family and community. I was pensive and curious at the hormonal rush that took place within me ushering in my exposure to love and my first girlfriend! I was confused at the disparity in the home situations of my friends—some families had a father around and some didn't, some were wealthy while some weren't, some lived in the more upscale parts of Barbados while many didn't. This became the source of many questions that vigorously swirled around in my mind.

When I turned 18, I had the opportunity of a lifetime. I remember anxiously opening the letter and reading aloud "Dear David Ricardo Inniss, it is with great pleasure that we inform you that you have been accepted into the United States Military Academy as a member of the Class of 1999."

I read the letter over and over, maybe ten times, to verify that it was intended for me. I checked and re-checked the address on the envelope. Was it addressed to David Inniss from St. Philip, Barbados? Yes, it was. WOW! USMA? WestPoint? New York? Military School? College degree? I was in a state of disbelief and my mind was racing. The emotions came at me like Class IV whitewater rapids. I felt pride in the fact that this kid from a little village in the central part of one of the smallest islands in the world be so bold as to apply and get accepted to the world's premiere military institution. Truth be told, this was the second year I had been engaged in the application process for WestPoint. The previous year, I initiated the selection process and was well into it when I decided to withdraw my application. You see, at the time, Barbados offered free undergraduate level education at the University of the West Indies (UWI). I contemplated having to leave my friends, family and familiarity and decided I was not ready to do this. I enrolled in UWI and began pursuing an undergraduate degree in Economics and

Computer Science. Toward the end of my first year in the program, it occurred to me that I would struggle to differentiate myself from the many students who also took advantage of the tertiary education offered by the Barbados government. Hesitantly, I decided to inquire about WestPoint again and recommit to the application process. A couple weeks later my completed packet was submitted and as the adage goes, the rest was history.

The weeks after my acceptance were fast and furious. As I prepared for my departure, I learned I was the first person from my country ever to attend WestPoint. I also learned that two of my best friends from secondary school and colleagues in the Barbados Cadet Corps, Kevin and Randy were accepted into the US Naval Academy and the US Coastguard academy respectively. There was a swirl of media interviews and meetings with prominent individuals—the most important one being the meet-and-greet with the Barbadian Prime Minister who voiced his pride in our admission and implored us to ensure that we finished the deal by graduating.

In the midst of my euphoria, I soon came to the sobering realization that all the relationships I had built would be strained and leaving the care and protection of my mother was far more difficult than I anticipated. I realized that my brother who was five years younger than me would have a role model and guiding force in his life yanked away pretty suddenly—something that would ultimately impact his drive and ambition.

Being The Dad I Never Had

When I departed from the Grantley Adams International Airport in Barbados in June 1995, I left behind all that I knew, a way of life I appreciated and routines I found comfortable. I left it all for an adventure—an unknown land, an unknown culture, among unknown people. So with the thud of that American Airlines jet's landing gear touching down on the tarmac at John F. Kennedy Airport came a tsunami of nervousness, fears, doubts and questions. As I touched US soil for the first time, I mentally processed a checklist of the only possessions I had with me, "2 pairs of pants – CHECK; 2 shirts – CHECK; 3 pairs of socks – CHECK; toiletries – CHECK."

So when I landed at JFK, with nothing other than one small 24"x12"x12" duffle bag, I was on my way to joining the Long Gray Line to embark on one of the toughest, most enjoyable and developmental experiences of my life. I was and will be forever grateful that I got to tread where the likes of Dwight Eisenhower, George Patton, Douglas MacArthur, Norman Schwarzkopf and Henry Flipper have trod. I am proud to have met people like Brian Smith, Matthew Tarjick, Ty Amey, Tom Tolman, Brian Reid and Jeff Braun who served with courage and have become great fathers and community leaders.

Being immersed in such a tough experience in a strange country forced me to grow up quickly. And I did. I felt the pressure as I learned more and more about the history of "this rockbound highland home", tucked neatly away on the banks of The Hudson River. I realized that the difficulty of admission to this institution paled in comparison to the absolute challenge of graduating.

33

Nevertheless, I was determined to do myself and my country proud on all fronts, particularly in terms of the four developmental pillars that were prioritized at "The Academy"— physical fitness, academic proficiency, military leadership and a commitment to the utmost level of integrity.

By the time I graduated as a Distinguished Cadet, I was in the best physical shape of my life. I rose to the academic challenge, having achieved a rank of #34 in my graduating class. I experienced first class military training and was exposed to some of the best leaders this world has ever seen. I was also spiritually sound with complete self-awareness. I believe that I truly "grew up" during my time at WestPoint.

My emotions at graduation were confusing. I was elated at having overcome all the obstacles that were placed before me. However, I also recall the overwhelming sadness that I felt upon graduation as I looked toward my future—a future that began with one of my lifelong dreams crushed. Despite my aspirations and intense preparation, my military officer career never materialized. This was devastating. I was convinced and wary that this utopian life I lived at USMA, where trust and honor were commonplace was gone forever and would be replaced by a "dog-eat-dog" world where everyone clamored for their own gain without regard for their fellow man or woman.

The disappointment of not realizing my lifelong dream of being an infantry officer was real! Although the outcome resulted from circumstances beyond my control, I still felt dejected. Watching my classmates on graduation day change from their WestPoint gray to US Army green and pin on their fresh lieutenant butter bars was a very sentimental moment for me. While they did that, I was changing into civilian attire and doing the ceremonial drive away, through the gates by the Thayer Hotel with WestPoint, the place where I became a man, in the rearview mirror.

Six months later, I landed in Sacramento where I began a career in the high tech world as a software engineer. I worked hard, honed my skills, sought mentors, and built a solid network. By my mid-20s, I was a homeowner, had completed a Master's degree, was actively mentoring youth in the community, and was doing extremely well in my career.

So, on my 30th birthday, the confusion peaked. It occurred to me that I had totally ignored the emotional toll of paternal apathy in my early years and father absence in my adolescent years. As a coping mechanism, I immersed myself in goal achievement. I didn't just "go to college," I had to go to WestPoint! I didn't just do well at WestPoint, I had to be a Distinguished Cadet! I had to be the first from my country to go there! I didn't just complete my Master's degree, I had to do so with nothing less than a 3.9 GPA! I set extremely challenging goals for myself and was an achievement junkie to soothe my emotional wounds.

Even though I gritted my teeth and pushed my way through life thus far, at that moment, the thoughts and questions would not go away. The questions were different from the ones that were in my head before. Before, I would ask myself riveting questions like "What was wrong with him? Why couldn't he love? Why did he choose to hit me so violently? Why did he choose alcohol over his family? Why was he such a difficult father?" But as I sat there, the questions shifted. Now, I asked "What was wrong with me? Why didn't he love me? Did I not deserve better? Was I the reason he seemingly rejected our family? Was I a difficult son?"

I was no longer able to use my old tactics of avoidance and immersion in achievement. I became depressed and quickly spiraled into the depths of anger and resentment. I became specifically sensitive to anything that looked like, smelled like or tasted like rejection! My male friends were few. Other than the long-term relationships I formed in my early high school years, I did not trust men...period. I passed up numerous opportunities for mentors because I couldn't ground myself in the belief that men I allowed in would not be malicious, disruptive, self-serving and disingenuous.

My struggles with relationships with women were under the spotlight as well. I developed an intense fear of their rejection. And while I considered myself a solid communicator, I realized I lacked the ability to effectively deal with confrontation and conflict. How did this manifest itself? Well, we all know the stages of any relationship. They all begin, regardless of the context, with a honeymoon stage. This stage is filled with infatuation and euphoria but soon ends when the participants come to terms with the realization that the "other person" is not perfect but is rather another human being with several flaws. Every time romantic relationships reached this point for me, I felt exposed. I described it as being like a caged lion! So majestic from a distance, but whilst caged, everyone peering in could see every flaw. That everyone could see every blemish on my hide, every scar that notched my face and the weather beaten dullness that came from the many previous battles was scary. That feeling of being exposed was uncomfortable for me and I found that I would shut down emotionally before anyone could really get close enough to reach the "heart of the lion."

Needless to say, the zip and pizzazz that were trademarks of a vibrant personality diminished. With time, the flash in my eyes waned until it was almost nonexistent. I could force a smile or two but those who knew me well could easily detect that they weren't genuine. The flame within—my flame—was quickly going out! In retrospect, I recognize many symptoms of depression and Post Traumatic Stress Disorder (PTSD) that I was unaware of at the time.

It took me what felt like an eternity to gain an understanding of this dark period and get back on the path toward a purposeful existence. Counseling sessions, personal reflection and shoring up my spiritual connection were just a few of the tools that were instrumental as I worked on my wholeness. Had I realized the extent to which the fatherless experience took a toll on my emotional and mental wellness, I would probably have made different decisions about how I handled it earlier in my life. I would probably have given it the attention it deserved and not avoided it as I did. But alas, there is hope yet!

Eight years and two sons later, I confront this travesty that affects thousands…millions of men worldwide with a restored voice and an energetic pen! I am making decisions daily that are focused on halting the generational perpetuation of fatherlessness in my family. I now live to speak passionately about father-absence, paternal apathy and fatherhood, sharing with anyone willing to listen about the devastating impact that the absence of an engaged father may have. It doesn't matter how long you defer it, how great your excuses are, or how well you can hide from it, the unanswered questions will invariably continue until you proactively deal with it.

As I made baby steps toward emotional closure, day-to-day events would simply throw me back. I found myself so open to learning but rather defensive about securing the approval as a "good" father. Having never experienced the affirmation of a father, I turned to my spouse. I, unfairly I might add, placed my insecurities squarely on her shoulders. That was undue pressure. My insecurities originated with my intense desire to be different for my family. I wanted my children to love me and revere me as a dad. I wanted my wife to love and respect me as a man and as a father of her children. I also had a strong desire for all of them to affirm my efforts to be different from those of the line of men that came before me in my family. All of this desire for affirmation, I would later learn was misplaced.

So, if you made it this far, it means I might just have your attention. As I shared my experience, at what points in time were you in the *Supporter* role? When did you find yourself nodding in acknowledgment or saying "I can relate to that?" When did the *Activator* voice in you kick in? Let's continue with our journey and identify the possible emotional impacts of fatherlessness.

Chapter 4
Lifelong Wounds

Throughout the conversations I have had with men about their perceptions of their fatherless experience, many believed their fatherless experience led to prolonged life challenges. The absence of a connected dad was not the only influential challenge they faced. Yet, the participants of the study traced some of the most challenging aspects of their lives back to some of the wounds they experienced as little boys without a solid model of male citizenship. Like I stated about me, the men they became were shaped by the wounds they incurred.

Among the beliefs fatherless men had about the prolonged impact of their experience was how the lifelong challenges showed up. Five of the most prominent forms of lifelong challenges as described by men who experienced fatherlessness are: early exposure to adult challenges, inability to cope with difficult times, susceptibility to involvement in deviant behaviors, difficulty with adult spousal relationships, and obsession with achievement.

While I have heard many life stories that illustrate the importance of the father-son relationship, none have been more profound than this experience I wish to share with you. At the time that this apparently insignificant situation unfolded, I had no clue how intensely it would influence my life. Ultimately, it ended up in tens of speeches, presentations and workshops, as it clearly illustrated several tenets about the impact of father loss.

The Writing on the Wall

A few years ago, I took an interest in growing a thriving real estate business. Although the country and world was coming back from one of the worst economic downturns in history that started in the real estate sector, I rationalized that the only place to go for real estate in the recovery was up! I got the education and training I needed, passed the requisite examinations and became a licensed realtor in the state of California. I looked forward to this new adventure! Challenging but rewarding, this decision literally opened the door to one of the most influential experiences of my adult life.

It was a beautiful spring day in North Highlands, California. The blue cloudless sky provided a wonderful backdrop that brought everything to life. Blossoming trees stood like sentries on either side of the streets. Some trees buzzed with excitement as thousands of bees got busy doing their work to keep the world's food chain in order. Birds chirped loudly as the distant roar of cars on a local freeway served as their backup bass line.

Upon learning of my recent foray into real estate, a friend asked if I would place one of her investment properties on the market. I was excited. With the accompaniment of one of my real estate mentors, I entered the home to determine what steps were necessary to prepare it for showing. The house was tucked away on a quiet street and was previously occupied by tenants who moved in and never paid a single month's rent. As a result, they were obviously evicted and the eviction process lasted almost four months. We were expecting the worst.

As we entered the home, our fears were confirmed. The house was a total disaster. The interior of the house looked as though a hand grenade was detonated there! We purposefully bypassed the living room and headed for the backyard. We would start there and work our way through to the front of the property to assess the damage. The yard was a mess. The once beautifully maintained pool was green, filled with algae and had several pieces of furniture floating in it. Garbage and litter was strewn everywhere. I could hardly believe what I was witnessing.

We reentered the house. I stood in the living room while my mentor went to the kitchen. I looked around in amazement before I heard a painful moan emerge from the kitchen. My mentor had pulled the door of the fridge only to find spoilt rotten meat abandoned in the unplugged refrigerator. The odor was mind blowing!

I began walking the rooms. I could smell the musty odor of an unkempt, untidy home. I noticed the graffiti that was left all over the walls—blue ink, black ink, red ink. Every single wall, from floor to ceiling, was covered in scribblings from a permanent marker. Apparently, the family that was evicted had used the walls as their communication platform. It was their very own oversized notepad on which they had scribbled numerous messages, phone numbers and addresses all over the white walls.

I walked slowly wondering about the restoration job that we would have to perform to prepare the house for sale. I entered one of the bedrooms that I presumed belonged to one of the children in the family and noticed that this room was also tagged with graffiti. As I was leaving the room, I noticed a paragraph in perfect penmanship in the middle of the wall.

"Writing on the Wall"

43

I was so moved by it that I whipped out my cell phone and snapped a photo, never realizing the impact that the message and the photo would have on many.

The message read:

"My Mom tried to raise us like suburban kids in the projects. She let me believe in Santa and all that crap. We had some man murdered a few doors down and the police didn't come and get his body till daylight the next day. Noon in fact..."

It continued.

"But Christmas and the yearlong anticipation of Santa coming to the projects was incredibly real to me...until I was about 6 years old. That's when my demands on Santa (aka my mama on food stamps) got a little too steep. I was like Dear Santa: where the heck is my daddy and my grand daddies?"

That note spoke volumes to me. It touched me at my very core as I could relate to the sadness and to an extent, the anger of that six-year-old boy. It immediately shot me back to the times when I, as a six-year-old boy experienced my "wounds." The same emptiness that drove that little boy to ask those questions, I experienced. His relationship with a heroic mother who secretly made it all happen in the household was one that I shared. His realization that he was parented by a single mother who made the most of very few resources was one that I too drew. We also had the common experience of knowing Santa and gifts at Christmas, despite the fact that our family operated with very modest means. But there was more beneath the surface in this message.

Several aspects of the father-absent experience were on display. The generational perpetuation of fatherlessness was clearly apparent. Notice that this little boy did not simply ask about his father. Instead, he painfully inquired, "Where the heck is my daddy and grand daddies?" He grew up without ever seeing any male member of his family tree willing to be present for their offspring. These questions, though described as a memory from a six-year old at the time, possibly surfaced several years after a more grown up, rational young man began to ponder about his life circumstances. This is rather typical. My experience, and that of many others, is that unanswered questions remain buried within the psyche and soul of un-fathered boys. Often they neither have the courage nor the belief that it is their place to ask such provocative questions until they are far older and increasingly disillusioned. Ultimately, these questions surface with resentment and anger as was the case in the writing on the wall and my own personal experience that I shared before.

Another factor about fatherlessness that was evident from this graffiti-laden wall is the notion of an environment of desensitization. Often, fatherless men who become fathers themselves describe growing up in environments in which families are completely desensitized to the necessity of a fathers' presence. In such environments, there are little to no expectations placed on men who fathered children. As a result, it almost became understood in some neighborhoods that fathers would leave and move on to their next big adventure, popping in periodically for a birthday party, to deliver a Christmas gift or to "drop off" some financial assistance upon the mother's request. No pressure was placed on men to actively participate in the rearing of their young ones.

I recall a scene in a recent movie in which an unwed mother and father of a two-year-old son were chatting. The father had just popped in for one of his periodic visits when mom asked him to take over caretaking for a week because she had to travel for a few days. His reaction was interesting. With eyes wide open, he sighed in disbelief. Through his body language, his thought process was clear. What do you mean take care of him for a week? That is not my job! As he shook his head, he responded "I don't know about that. I can possibly do two days but I can't do that for the whole week!"

This is an example of the mindset that a desensitized environment cultivates. The hesitation from the mother in asking and the disbelief by the father in what was being asked of him speak volumes about this mentality. This same attitude was confirmed for me by one gentlemen who described his early-adult attitude toward engagement with his children by exclaiming "Me? That's what moms and grandmas do!"

The numbness to father absence is typical in many of our communities most devastated from generations of absent fathers. Belief systems, perceptions about being a man, and thoughts on what is acceptable male citizenship are primarily shaped by the mothers and grandmothers who stay. Normally, in such environments, crime, violence and masculine negativity are all prominent societal realities. Men are seemingly given a pass, allowing them to circumvent their paternal responsibilities to teach, guide and influence the character development of their children. At the core of influencing true change that alters the tide of rampant paternal neglect is the need to identify and eliminate elements of this desensitization to the importance of fathers.

The Activator in Me

This story, though simple in how it unfolded, captures the complexity of a serious phenomenon that impacts the fabric of the global society in which we live. It is imperative that we take heed of the proverbial "writing on the wall" and begin to make significant efforts in reshaping the existence of our sons. This starts with you! It starts with every father who has the responsibility of grooming another young man and preparing him for manhood. It must be initiated by a worldwide body of fathers who are committed to introspection and changes in their approaches to fathering. They must be willing to unpack traditionally held views of masculinity, question them and ensure that healthy perceptions of masculinity are passed on to the future generations. This enlightened core of dads must internalize the notion and obligation to father in such a way that their grandchildren have no choice but to boast of a line of responsible men who were present both emotionally and physically.

Now that would be a shift, wouldn't it? Are you a part of this body committed to change? I am assuming you are since you are still here in the conversation.

Chapter 5
Prepare a Legacy

One of the highest priorities expressed to me by men who grew up without a father is to create a different life story for their offspring—leaving a legacy that their children could pass on to future generations. Like them, I consider this to also be a central reason for my very existence. I too am committed to this concept, admittedly to the point of being obsessed with "leaving a legacy" for my sons. But what exactly is a legacy? And what do we really mean when we talk about having or leaving a legacy? Can a legacy be negative? And if so, can one alter a legacy, and reshape, retool or create a new one if a negative one is what he/she inherited? How is this idea of "legacy" related to a father's capacity to dramatically alter the frame of reference for many subsequent generations in his family tree?

49

CHAPTER 5 Prepare a Legacy

Let's start with putting together a framework of what makes a legacy. The term is often loosely thrown around and means different things to different people. For the purpose of this book, let us put some parameters around its definition so we will share a common definition and speak about it from a uniform viewpoint. Webster defines a legacy as something received from a predecessor. It is also defined as something that connotes how someone is remembered or the body of contributions they made during their life. Another source indicated that a legacy is something taken from one period and passed down to another period. Yet another source stated that having a legacy is tantamount to allowing something that originated with one's ancestors to spread among people freely and naturally.

Families often pass family heirlooms and other material items from generation to generation. Such material assets are predominantly referred to as an inheritance. You can touch, hold, feel and physically store these tangible inherited items. The term legacy, on the other hand, is more prominently reserved for describing immaterial, cultural norms that are bridged across a time period or generation. It has more to do with the act of transitioning one's learnings and less on passing on one's earnings. It is less focused on how you pass on valuables to another generation and more about how you pass on values. It elevates the transition of principles for positive living over possessions. It prioritizes the value of morals instilled from one generation to another over money. It is about sharing a "way of being" and less about wealth. It places more on the value of inherited self-love than an actual inheritance.

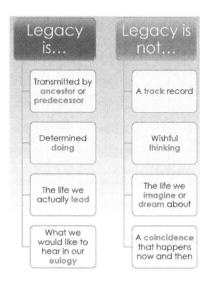

Legacy is...	Legacy is not...
Transmitted by ancestor or predecessor	A track record
Determined doing	Wishful thinking
The life we actually lead	The life we imagine or dream about
What we would like to hear in our eulogy	A coincidence that happens now and then

In general, the successful creation of a legacy requires the person attempting to create the legacy to be crystal clear about what he/she wishes to pass on to the next generations. Often, individuals wanting to create or leave a legacy are overwhelmingly committed to making a meaningful, sustainable and uplifting contribution to mankind through the recognition that a particular cause is greater than they are. The commitment to this greater cause drives legacy creators to practice responsible behaviors that ensure that their way of life outlives their existence.

Now, let's circle the wagons back and relate this idea of legacy to the fatherless experience. Every single fatherless father with whom I spoke (and I have met hundreds) described an intense desire to create a new reality for their sons and daughters. This intense desire remained intact even if the fathers had already fallen short of this lofty goal by the time we had our conversation.

Regardless of their level of success thus far at living according to this desired legacy, they spoke of giving their children opportunities with a present and engaged father. These were opportunities that they themselves never experienced. Although I lived this, I always found it rather impressive and a powerful gesture that one would be so committed to giving someone something that one never had or knew. The other side of the coin of this lofty intention is one that tells the story of the pressure it could place on the individual trying to create a new legacy for men in his family.

Although fatherless men may have some fantastic intentions, I contend that we still operate from a position of deficit—a position of never seeing behaviors modeled to us that we are trying to give to others. As a result, we are left prone to rely on repeated trial and error, often fathering with more errors than we would be willing to admit. A modified version of the game of Marco Polo comes to mind, with one individual wading around blindfolded in a dark room as he follows the moving voice of other person he is trying to locate. Of course, many may argue that these are lessons we can learn from the numerous father-substitutes we tend to adopt—the uncles, the coaches, the pastors, the teachers, the counselors, the military, the church, etc. The general consensus, however, among men who have lived this is that having those lessons from our biological fathers would be preferred and more impactful.

There are several implications of the dilemma that surround creating a legacy that we never experienced. Foremost, it means we have to be intentional, logical and methodical about how we go about preparing for and creating the new experiences we wish to pass on to our sons' and daughters' generations and even beyond.

I am frequently quoted as saying, "fathers will often father in the way they were fathered!" So, the un-fathered men, or those who had exposure to apathetic fathering, start with the disadvantage of having had a negative model or in extreme cases, no model at all. Consequently, they are more likely, by their own admission, to repeat behaviors that contribute to what I label as "the daddy issue"—a lack of emotional and psychological balance that results from the absence of a father, the abuse of a paternal relationship or paternal unreliability. Equal in importance is that these behaviors may contribute to the generational perpetuation of fatherlessness. Model-less fathering leaves us exposed to mistakes and consequences that we could have been more prepared to deal with had we had the presence of an in-person guide.

Hearing the quote "fathers will often father in the way they were fathered," you may be tempted to jump to the conclusion that I have little faith in our ability as fatherless men to become phenomenal dads. Not true! The mere fact that I wrote this book speaks to my unwavering belief that in spite of our circumstances, we can rise to the occasion for our children. There is a second part to the quote that goes like this:

"Fathers will father in the way they were fathered…unless they boldly stand up, challenge their circumstances and with intentionality commit to creating a new legacy for their children."

The quote, in its entirety, is the foundation on which my belief that we can be the dads we never had is grounded. Success at achieving this requires you to be bold. It demands that you have faith in your ability. It asks that you demonstrate perseverance and a willingness to never quit on the fatherhood journey. It challenges you to come to terms with the role you can play in altering the course of your family history. YOU can do it! YOU have what it takes! Your children's future can be changed by YOU!

Needless to say, the fact that you are still reading this book right now suggests to me that you are already being bold about making a difference. Why do you have to take such "bold" action? Why do you have to be so committed? Why does it require such determination? Well, over the course of the last few years as I studied this topic, one of the realizations that struck me is that parenting/fathering is hard! It is not for the faint-hearted! Unlike any other activity, it challenges you to elevate your performance in every facet of your life every single day. Imagine you are a potter, entrusted with this highly valuable lump of clay. You mount it onto the potter's wheel and start to shape it. Every single move you make matters! The clay will respond to every movement of your fingers as you shape the clay into something valuable. This analogy gives some insight into the skill and difficulty of fathering, but it also speaks to the sensitivity and impact of our actions as fathers.

Even with all of the stars aligned, fathering is by far one of the most physically, emotionally and mentally draining roles that a man can perform. A close friend of mine relayed a scenario to me recently that I thought captured the daunting feeling that some men experience as they approach fathering. She described being a relatively solid athlete at her high school where she dominated internal track meets. Her signature was the fact that she preferred to run barefoot and had achieved significant success doing so. Well, as expected she was chosen to represent her school at a regional track meet. She recalled showing up at the starting blocks in her regular physical education uniform only to notice that all the other competitors were decked out in high-end performance wear complete with the matching outer wear. They all had the latest technology in sprinting footwear—light, colorful with the track-gripping spikes across the front half of each shoe. She described the feeling of fear, doubt and inadequacy that overtook her at that moment. Certainly, her confidence was shaken. My friend, stood there feeling underdressed, under-equipped, under-prepared and overwhelmed. At the end of the race, the results were not in her favor. Her key lesson, she acknowledged, was the idea that more and more is required as the stakes get higher.

The stakes are seldom higher than those at play for fathering. A whole lot is on the line. So when we show up at the metaphorical starting line, and realize we are under-exposed, under-modeled and in many ways under-prepared, it is not uncommon for the feelings of despair and hopelessness to set in. Truth be told, the temptation to not even run in the race may be pretty strong except that your name was already announced over the PA system and all eyes are on you. Now, you must follow through. Even in your crappy-looking PE uniform and your bare feet! It is at this moment when it feels highly intimidating that your "boldness" is required. While you bring the bold desire in order to make a difference, you must also focus on constantly upgrading your equipment to match the stakes of the race you are in. It is my intention that this book delivers some of that high-end, research-based, performance-enhancing "equipment" you will need to maintain your edge and excel in "the race."

Remember, "Fathers will father in the way they were fathered…unless they boldly stand up, challenge their circumstances and with intentionality commit to creating a new legacy for their children."

The intentionality required in the quote indicates that totally shifting the way of life for generations of men in your family tree demands focused, on-purpose preparation. I would even go as far as to say that the health and sustainability of your family relies on it. In my consulting practice, I often taught organizations ways to create sustainable change in their organizations by altering embedded belief systems. It is no surprise to me that the same methodologies I teach to organizations who are pursuing sustainable, long-lasting, adaptive change are applicable to the un-fathered man attempting to make similar change in his family. Comparable approaches will only serve to benefit the fatherless man who is attempting to trade the generational plight of father-absence for a legacy of enriching, fully present fathering in his family.

Focused, On-Purpose Preparation for Your Legacy

I classify the journey on which we embark as fatherless fathers as a spiral-like one, that if done well, sees us forever "going up" as we elevate our effectiveness as fathers. The journey, as I mentioned before, is characterized by periods of exploration, and growth—neither of which take place without some pain. The pain factor requires us to demonstrate resiliency and focus on complete restoration as we grow into the fathers we hope to be—the dads we never had.

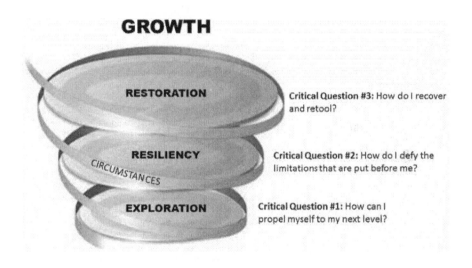

GROWTH

RESTORATION — Critical Question #3: How do I recover and retool?

RESILIENCY — Critical Question #2: How do I defy the limitations that are put before me?

CIRCUMSTANCES

EXPLORATION — Critical Question #1: How can I propel myself to my next level?

The illustration above highlights this concept of what it takes to be prepared for your legacy. You must be willing and able to explore, go after new things, discover what was unknown to you, broaden your perspectives, be open to new knowledge, break down barriers, etc. This exploration requires humility, since you must buy into the truth that you don't know everything and have a lot to learn. The openness to exploration of new things alone is not sufficient, however. Numerous barriers and situations, perceived and real, will continually punctuate your journey. You will have numerous opportunities to give in and quit as some of these circumstances may feel like they are purposed to take you out. However, you will also have many chances to persevere, demonstrating the resiliency necessary for legacy-creation. It may feel, along this journey that each time you recover from a knock down, you attempt to get up, and something else knocks you flat again.

This repeated cycle of being knocked over, and getting up can be frustrating and depleting. Nevertheless, mustering the wherewithal to recover and actually doing it can be the most rewarding part of the journey. Repeatedly demonstrating resiliency and recovering from setbacks strengthens us and prepares us for the next challenge. Through this process of repeated restoration, we meet head on the experiences and disadvantages we had and refuse to allow them to impact the new legacy we are creating.

Unfortunately for us, life does not stop throwing us curveballs simply because we were able to overcome a round of difficulty and experience growth and restoration. Life somehow does not allow us to be stagnant once we have grown. Instead, it is within our human nature to look forward and strive for higher heights. So, we end up exploring again, breaking more barriers and progressing toward more growth. By now, your mind should be racing about your next few explorations as a father or simply as a person. You should be intensely considering the legacy for your children.   Here is a legacy assignment for you:

1. Think about the legacy you wish to leave
2. Record it—write it down in a journal or special place, keep an audio recording of it
3. Share it with others you trust if you are comfortable doing so.
4. Describe it as what you REALLY want and are considering and see what others think.
5. Review it on a regular basis—do a self-audit to assess if you are on track
6. Revise it as necessary—it is yours!

With your desired legacy as a father in hand, we are ready to look at some practical steps to thriving after your fatherless experience. We are ready to dig deep into our practical steps for becoming the Dad you never had. I'm excited! Are you?

Chapter 6 - Lesson #1
Establish the Contract

A pervasive theme throughout this book is the idea that "the missing model" is one of the most impactful consequences of father absence or paternal neglect. Trying to be an outstanding dad for your children without the experience of a close, respected model of positive fathering requires that we approach parenting with thoughtfulness, introspection, resourcefulness and a willingness to learn. As fatherless boys, we grow up engrossed in what seems like a never-ending search for substitutes. Since many of us view the primary role of a father as that of "teacher," we long for places where we can find those lessons that were never taught to us by our dads. Unfortunately, the father-substitutes we pursued and invariably selected were not always upstanding. The model void that comes with the terrain of fatherlessness is fertile soil in which misguided beliefs about manhood, masculinity, fatherhood, discipline, emotional expression and nurturing behaviors can take root.

By the time we transition into adulthood, we have typically encountered a variety of impactful circumstances, and influential people. Coaches, teachers, family members, church leaders, managers and mentors are just a few who pour into us, inspiring us in many ways to be good fathers. They attempt to guide us in areas like career exposure, educational accomplishments, professional development, marriage and spousal relationships, spirituality and physical wellness—all of which, according to numerous fatherless men, are the areas most impacted by the absence of the father-teacher. This positive exposure to oneself as a man and father with valuable life skills may contradict other misguided perceptions about manhood or fatherhood that we may have picked up along the way.

Often, our desire to be different to our sons than our fathers were to us motivates us to accept these new approaches that we learn over time. For many of us, however, embracing the new approaches to fathering and living out our lives as men is not trivial. In fact, it can be quite challenging. In my conversations with fatherless fathers, many spoke positively of new insights they picked up as they transitioned through adulthood and additions to their value system that influenced how they fathered. Can you relate to this? Have you had a mixture of experiences that led to an earlier approach fathering that you later dismissed and replaced with a newly "discovered" strategy? Did you have (or used to have) a natural response in certain situations with your sons that was rooted in the misguided perceptions about fatherhood you developed early in your transition to manhood? Was this "natural response" healthy?

While talking to fatherless men who were parents themselves, I questioned them to discuss their response when faced with the scenario of an emotionally shaken son who was crying. After much discussion, they universally concluded that although their upbringing taught them that "boys are tough" and "boys don't cry," their broadened exposure led them to develop an acquired sensitivity toward their sons' emotional freedom. The natural response in such a scenario was one of quickly and harshly questioning why their son was crying and recommending it be stopped right away. However, by pausing and reflecting through the lens of enlightened experiences and a reshaped value system, they have become more measured in their response and focused on nurturing their sons' ability to describe emotions.

Does it describe you as well? I know that this hits home for me. I refer to the conflict between the learned values embraced in the early stages of the fatherless experience and the values we acquire as we mature and gain more exposure as The Conflict of Learned Behaviors. It is at the root of the seven tips that are captured in this book. The tips are purposefully designed to inject the measured, well thought out responses into the scenarios we will encounter as fathers. A key part of intercepting the natural responses in various situations is to clearly establish up front the type of fathers we want to be. What do you plan on doing as a dad? How will you approach these tasks? Who are others who can affect or are affected by your actions?

This leads me to introduce Lesson #1 – Establish the Fatherhood Contract. As you attempt to shape how you will empower your children with a life experience that differs from yours, one of the first steps is to conceptualize the values and details that will guide you. It is not sufficient to simply conceptualize these details. They should be written down. A great friend once told me "A goal without a plan is worth nothing but a plan without action is worth even less." I agree but I also know from experience that goals are more effective when we write them down.

On March 24, 2007, I paced impatiently along the hallway outside the hospital room where my wife was in labor with our firstborn son. She had already spent close to 40 hours of feeling ill and was desperately ready for the delivery to be over. By now, she was pretty disheveled, her face pale from nausea and eyes bloodshot from the lack of sleep.

Now my wife was a rather detail-oriented woman. Prior to her arrival at the hospital, she followed the instructions of the pre-natal care nurses to the letter. She took every supplement she was supposed to take, followed the exercise regimen they recommended and even rehearsed the correct breathing patterns we learned in Lamaze class. She had constructed a thorough—and I mean thorough—birth plan in which she expressed all of her desires as to how she wanted the birth of our first baby to go. Foremost on her list was the desire to have no use of pain relieving drugs at all. I would often overhear her talking to her friends and suggesting that she really wanted to "do this thing au natural." She also stated she did not want any drugs used to induce labor or speed up the process. She wanted contractions and the delivery of the baby to flow naturally. The birth plan also instructed delivery room nurses to place the baby on my wife's chest immediately after birth. The intent was to take advantage of that immediate post-birth moment of mother-son bonding that my wife had read about during her preparation for child birth.

I truly admired how organized she was. In fact, I joined in the focus on details by having a hospital-ready bag packed and in each of our cars a full month prior to our planned due date. Well the night of March 22nd is when the pre-labor "festivities" began. It started with extreme nausea and the feeling of contractions. Now admittedly, I was known for having grand ideas and establishing big visions and not for meticulously dealing with minute details. But, for this delivery situation, I read extensively about everything.

I knew the contractions my wife was experiencing were different from the Braxton Hicks contractions she had experienced periodically over the past month. (Yes, I knew what the difference was and I am extremely proud of it!) I broke out my personal hospital readiness kit which included a notepad, a pen, a copy of my wife's birth plan and a stopwatch. And there I was timing the contractions with a stop watch around my neck like a varsity coach.

"Starting again!" she would wince.

"Ready, go!" was my response as I started the stop watch. I remained engaged with that watch until the contraction was over.

"Okay, it stopped" was my cue to stop the stopwatch, record the length of the contraction, and reset the watch to capture the time between the contractions. I had this thing down and our teamwork was impeccable that night.

As the time between contractions got smaller and smaller, I contacted the Advice Nurse and explained the precision timing and the nausea. The events so far had completely changed our perception of how smooth this process was going to be. After listening to me, she uttered the words that I was waiting for.

"I think you guys should head on in."

"Okay" I responded with excitement and started the routine we had rehearsed. We operated like firemen at the station that had just received a 911 call. The car was pre-packed and we were out of the house and on the way to the hospital in less than five minutes.

The birth was complicated. I watched slowly as my wife's birth plan was repeatedly compromised. Her desire for no pain medication was the first to go as her extreme nausea and associated pain resulted in a recommendation for an epidural. Labor unexpectedly slowed down and after more than 25 hours in labor, it was recommended labor be sped along via the labor-progressing drug Pitocin. That was the second birth plan item that was shot down. As the delivery took place, it was determined that my son had the umbilical cord wrapped around his neck and was being periodically choked. As I stood next to my wife, held her hand and encouraged her, I watched with joy as my son was born and with absolute horror as the nurses held him, cut the umbilical cord and quickly whisked him away to the neonatal intensive care unit. That was it! Nothing on the birth plan occurred. I left my wife and joined the nurses in the NICU.

I peered through the glass into the NICU unit, watching my son. There was a love there I had never experienced before. I watched the rise and fall of his chest. I looked at every feature that his ten-minute-old body had to see if there were any similarities to "his daddy." And as I looked on while he peacefully slept, I began to mutter under my breath.

"I will never fail you."

"I promise never to leave you."

"I will teach you anything you need to know."

"I will make sure that you know how much you are loved."

My son Jalen Omari made it through these initial scares and has never ceased to deliver on the joy he promised. As we waited over the next two and a half days in the care of the post-natal medical team, I decided to put into writing all of those things I wanted to do and be for my son. I wrote it in the form of a contract—a binding agreement between Jalen and me. I wrote it as a document that both Jalen and I could use to periodically check in on my approaches to fathering. Was I defaulting regularly to some of the misguided lessons that came naturally to me as a result of my fatherless and model-less experience? Or was I striding in my learned knowledge about daddying and exhibiting the patience and situational awareness necessary to overcome the natural response?

My goal for putting this contract into writing was to create a mechanism that would help me make the unnatural my new natural. I infused intentionality into everything I did as a father by documenting a checklist by which anyone could evaluate my progress and either say "well done" or check me when I fell short. I wanted my sons to know I took the privilege of being their dad very seriously.

Read on to see the Fatherhood Contract I wrote as I waited for my first son to be released from the hospital. I adopted it twenty months later for my second son Nico. Now, why is this written contract important? Aren't these things obvious? Some of you may even state that you already do these things naturally. Regardless, the truth is that some of us don't.

Remember what I described as the Conflict of Learned behaviors? In our jobs, many of us have checklists of things to do that we keep on our desks or white boards. Some of us have electronic checklists that we use to guide us through our day, ensuring we do not miss anything. When we attempt to do home improvement projects, we develop a list of things we need, tools required and tasks we need to complete in order to make the project an overwhelming success. In the grand scheme of things, is a home improvement project or a task list for work more or less important than the relationship you hope to build with your children? Are the items on these lists that we so readily create going to have life-lasting impact? I would venture to say "No!"

So, if we are willing to place such energy in home projects and work projects, shouldn't we be willing to create a similar list for the most important job that we will do as men? Are we fearful of writing this because it means it is something we must live by? But isn't that the point anyway? This contract is between you and your child. It is not a perfection pill! While you may fall short sometimes, you will always have this contract as a tool to calibrate where you are and provide some hints of what your next few actions ought to be.

Are you convinced yet? Do know what should be in your contract? The content of your Fatherhood Contract is a very personal thing. It relies on what you actually want to convey to your little one and what you want to measure about your performance as a dad. Nevertheless, I offer you a few suggestions to guide your thought process:

- Who are you going to commit to being in the context of your family unit?
- How are you going to deal with emotionality in your children?
- Do you plan on being transparent as far as your own emotionality is concerned?
- What will you do to help them develop academically?
- What level of importance will you place on their multifaceted development (i.e. educational, athletic, and spiritual, etc.)?
- What opportunities will you strive to provide for them?

- How will you demonstrate and teach them about resilience and their ability to recover from challenges that life throws their way?
- How will they know you love them?
- Why should they even believe that you love them?
- Is there a spiritual base on which you would like to build your relationship with your family?

I took these guidelines into account years ago when I first constructed my Fatherhood Contract. I ensured that mine described how I wanted to operate in the context of a family unit. I made sure it talked about my desire to be nurturing and to celebrate my family's emotional identity. It covered how I wanted to be a model—through my candor about both my successes and my failures. It talked about the little things that as a father I wanted to teach my boys—how to fly kites, ride bikes, throw balls—as well as the big things for which I wanted to be a reliable resource. It captured my approach to emotional expression and my vigilance for places in which I could hurt them in ways in which I myself was hurt.

I had one of the most rewarding experiences regarding this contract. At a local counseling center for men, I left a poster of my contract for the men who attended to see. It received lots of attention and, according to the owner of the center, many men attempted to establish their contracts as a result. I took my sons on a visit to that counseling center and years after I first wrote it, the poster was still on the wall in the main lobby. Faded into the background of the contract was a picture of my tiny baby boy Jalen with my hand on his

69

chest. I remember creating that poster. The owner, in a conversation with my sons, explained that it was the Fatherhood Contract that I created for them.

Now, I had revisited this contract tens of times over the years to gauge how I was doing but never with my sons who were too young to read it or understand its importance. This time, they were able to read it with me; we went through tenet by tenet and they told me how they thought I did. My sons' perception of me was heart-warming and the fact that they had concrete measures via which to communicate these perceptions was beneficial. Again, their commentary suggested I had some work to do but now, their feedback was pointed and specific. The contract did exactly what it was intended to do.

There are no truly valuable relationships that are not governed by some implicit or explicit agreement. Since fatherhood is by far one of the most important roles that men will play in today's world, why not make your agreement an explicit one. It is never too late to get your contract written, reviewed with your children and signed. Let's Go! This is just the beginning. Review my Fatherhood Contract and let's see what Lesson #2 reveals to us.

In accordance with my personal values and my commitment to true fatherhood, I do hereby enter into this contract with Jalen and Nico this 24th day of March in the year 2007, and this 29th day of November in the year 2008.

1. I will love, honor and respect your mother
2. I will love you unconditionally at all times
3. I will nurture and protect you from danger to the best of my abilities
4. I will provide for you, ensuring that you are always appropriately clothed, well fed and have a roof over your head
5. I will teach you how to ride a bicycle, throw a ball, and fly a kite
6. I will read to you
7. I will make sure that you attend schools that give you the greatest opportunity to excel
8. I will partner with your teachers to help you as much as I possibly can with school
9. I will be candid with you about my mistakes in life so that you can avoid the pitfalls that I fell into
10. I will reveal to you, in a non-boastful manner, the characteristics that I have that helped me overcome many challenges and achieve a level of "success"
11. I will help you to define success in terms that are suited to you
12. I will assist you in any way possible to help you achieve that success described above
13. I will be a tough disciplinarian at times, but this is out of love, and based upon my desire to fulfill everything else in this contract
14. I will **never** strike you
15. I will play with you
16. I will laugh with you
17. I will empathize when you cry during tough times, support you and show you that you can recover from any knock down
18. I will be strong enough to provide guidance but mild enough to encourage you
19. I will be firm enough to instill discipline, but flexible enough to show the value of tolerance
20. I will be attentive enough to recognize moments when I can potentially wound you and courageous enough to do what it takes to avoid them
21. I will be fearless enough to be wild in a Godly way and transfer that wildness to you my little boy

Signed: _____

Date: <u>03/24/2007, 11/29/2008</u>

Chapter 7 - Lesson #2
Build Resilient Qualities

Establishing a solid contract with your children, though a great first step to effective fathering, cannot be performed in isolation. As fatherless individuals, we may be challenged in many ways that our counterparts who were properly fathered are better prepared to navigate. We discussed the importance of a positive model before and the reason why I place such weight on the model is the validity of the "reproduction of fatherhood." This idea that we naturally reproduce the type of fathering we experienced when we become fathers unless we are intentional in all our actions toward being different is pretty powerful. Researchers before me have shown that key antecedents to father involvement are the attitudes and memories a father has about his experience as the beneficiary of paternal involvement or the victim of paternal apathy.

The evidence from research strongly indicates that fathers like us who enter adulthood having experienced a lack of paternal involvement or father absence are at a marked disadvantage over our dual-parented peers. Void of a solid paternal model of effective practices for a socially, emotionally, and cognitively healthy adult life, we are in turn prone to perpetuate the negativity of our experience on to our children, especially our sons.

When a father's attitudes and memories originate in an experience dominated by paternal apathy or abandonment, he must overcome his experiential influence to be engaged, available, accessible, and responsible with his offspring. Overcoming a lack of positive paternal modeling and avoiding the negative outcomes typically associated with it are both challenging and complex. Although several factors are at play, our capacity for resilience is a key determinant of our success at overcoming these challenges.

So what is resilience? In my own perusal of the information out there, I have found several definitions, all of which are relevant to the discussion we are having. First of all, most definitions indicate that resilience is a process meaning it is a series of actions or steps aimed at achieving a particular end state. This also suggests that resilience is initiated by a particular event and that you can develop and hone it over time, just as you can with any other process.

A second commonality among the definitions of resiliency is the fact that it encompasses positive adaptation. This simply refers to how we respond when events require us to be resilient. A third component of the definition is the presence of significant adversity, stressors or risks. The initiating event that forces us to adapt must pose sufficient risk to us, cause significant stress or adversely impact our lives in such a way that adaptation is required.

What personal and interpersonal gifts and strengths can we access within ourselves so we can grow through our experiences of adversity? To bring this question closer to home, how can we manifest increasing competence at fathering even in the face of significant challenges? How does the concept of resilience overlap with exposure to fatherlessness and its outcomes?

As I mentioned, the foundational judgments of resilience are (1) exposure to threat, risk, or severe adversity; and (2) the achievement of positive adaptation and competence in the face of such adversity. Let's see how this applies.

There are numerous published reports that assert that many of the social issues facing societies are rooted in fatherlessness. At a minimum, the perception of adversity and risks is therefore evident. Researchers have also found evidence to suggest that individuals exposed to similar risks and stressors can have highly differentiated outcomes. Individuals from disastrous backgrounds are able to develop high levels of competency and become emotionally, socially, and psychologically healthy while others fail to positively adapt under

74

similar circumstances. The same holds true for those of us who have experienced the absence of our fathers.

Over time, resilience and the study of resilience have shifted. In fact, there were three waves of thought about resilience that will be beneficial to those of us striving to overcome and achieve. The first wave of inquiry into resilience viewed it from the perspective of the negative conditions that caused psychological and emotional stressors to occur. In other words, the emphasis was initially placed on the adversity and stressors. As more attention was placed on the topic, focus shifted away from the negative factors that caused disruptions to determining how people adapted in the face of adversity. The emphasis placed on adaptation and how individuals thrived in the face of adversity paved the way for inquiry into how individuals develop resilient qualities like self-esteem, confidence, assuredness, and self-efficacy.

Most recent studies of resilience position it as "a motivational force within every person that drives them to pursue self-actualization and reintegration after life-disruptions." To understand why some of us behave differently in response to or deal better with the lack of a paternal model, we must unpack some of the individual characteristics and the process by which some of us acquired them. Additionally, identifying what factors serve as motivational forces that enable some to cope better after the experience of fatherlessness may shed light on what really drives some of our behaviors. For now, let us take an even deeper look into resilience to better game plan some strategies for building resilient qualities.

Several years ago, the four researchers Richardson, Neiger, Jensen, and Kumpfer collaborated and proposed a resilience model. This model resonated with me as it showed how people experiencing stressful or adverse circumstances can consciously or unconsciously drive outcomes. The following model is a variation of the Richardson Resilience Model. It is a simplification but preserves the gist of the original model. According to the model, life provides numerous perceived stressors, traumatic events and sources of adversity. As we experience our reality and adapt to our life situations, we develop a comfort zone—status quo for our spirit, body and mind. This comfort zone is not perfect but purely reflects how we operate in our normal form of existence.

Disruptions are events that knock us from our comfort zone, forcing us to adapt. Throughout our lives, we are barraged by

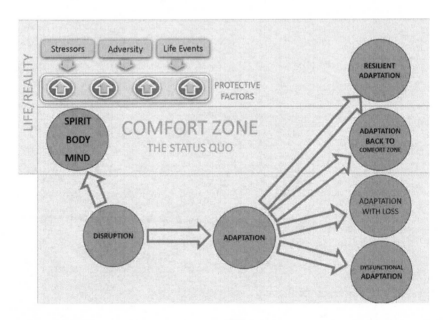

disruptions—internal or external—that constantly threaten our status quo and serve as major causes of stress. Repeated exposure to these stressors results in the formulation of resilient qualities as we try to protect our comfort zone and way of life. These qualities are depicted in the model as the protective factors that buffer life's adversities and help us maintain our place of comfort.

Expectedly, we don't have a protective factor for every form of adversity we encounter. As a result, our comfort zone is frequently compromised. Based on the model, when we face adversity, we adapt in one of four ways. When we experience resilient adaptation, we develop insight and further develop resilient qualities that serve as protective factors in the future. Sometimes, when faced with a disruption, we opt to simply move beyond the disruption, avoid changing and return to the status quo—our comfort zone. On some occasions, we decide to cut our losses, while on others we immerse ourselves in disruptive behaviors—dysfunctional adaptation.

So, now that we understand the model of resilience, let's apply it to our experiences and try to understand some of our differentiated responses to the stressors of fatherlessness. The spectrum of behavioral responses ranges from resilient adaptation through which we take actions to enhance our own fathering competence to dysfunctional adaptation, in which we turn to behaviors that further damage our families. We are increasingly aware of our natural responses to the child-rearing scenarios we encounter and the conflict between those natural responses and the more effective methods we learn. Remember this Conflict of Learned

Behaviors from the previous chapter? As we practice resilient forms of adapting to adversity, we further enhance the body of resilient qualities that we possess resulting in personal growth and improvement.

Some of us also respond to adversity and the risks associated with fatherhood with behaviors that cause us to incur significant losses. The absence or apathy of our fathers serves as a major source of frustration and disappointment. The sheer complexity of fathering under sometimes trying circumstances only adds to this. Combined, these stressors can lead us to less than ideal behavioral responses. Paternal neglect or abandonment of our own offspring fall into this category of responses. Should we choose to deal with adversity in this way, the losses we choose to absorb may be huge! Based on the pervasiveness of generational fatherlessness, it seems clear that many respond to the fear and stress of being a father with abandonment, apathy or neglect.

Another response is immersion in dysfunction. This is as an approach to salve the wounds we experienced in childhood and during the transition from boyhood to manhood. While this may include substance abuse, it also takes the form of other dysfunctional behaviors. Examples include anger outbursts, infidelity, and other actions rooted in the inability to trust others.

So, as obvious as it may seem, we have choices! That is exciting to me! Why? Well, it further cements my claim that we— you and I—can create the change that will alter generations ahead. If you are reading this book, it means there is probably some internal force within you that is pushing you to tackle the stress resulting from your direct or indirect experience with paternal neglect. To help in your own development of resilient qualities, I have come up with a list of practical things that have helped me with developing my own resilient responses to fatherhood stressors.

1. Accept that your experience occurred—acknowledge that the father absence or paternal apathy you experienced was a significant aspect of your life. Often there is a lot of pain and that "a" word—anger—may have been with you for a long time.

2. Be candid about your feelings around your experience. It took me a while to really admit that I was really devastated by the failed relationship I had with my father. I needed an outlet by which I could express the rush of emotions that flowed from me when I realized how widespread my own personal pain was. I took to journaling. I wrote how I felt then, how I was currently feeling and how I wanted to feel about the entire issue.

3. Have the imaginary conversation that you have always wanted to have with your father by writing him a letter. Ask the questions you have always wanted to ask. Many of them have probably gone unanswered for years. Express the conclusions that you were left to draw in his absence, physical or emotional. Tell him about the places and the times you really needed him—the games you competed in, the track meets you ran in, the presentations you did, the awards you received—all in his absence.

4.   Seek professional help as necessary. There is absolutely nothing wrong with soliciting the professional assistance of a counselor, therapist or life coach. We too often refuse to "subject ourselves" to any of these services because we assume they somehow diminish our ability to handle our own problems. There is no greater fallacy. Seeking the professional guidance of others after having what I consider to be a long term and rather traumatic experience is in fact the responsible thing to do. Several of the fatherless men I have met who have gone on to become outstanding fathers and upstanding men acknowledge that they had to "spend some time on the couch" to just hear their own pain, share their pain and use various proven techniques to assist with their healing. Upon my own acknowledgement of the impact fatherlessness had on me, I sought the help of several professionals and continue to go for frequent "tune ups" even to this day.

5.   Identify and believe in your strengths. Throughout our fatherless experience from boyhood into manhood, we have numerous questions. Sometimes the subject of these questions force us to question our responsibility for our own experience. As an example, I recall the experience I described earlier when on my 30th birthday, the questions I had asked for so many years shifted. I no longer questioned the responsibility of my father in our failed relationship but questioned my own role in it. What was wrong with the six-year-old me, the eight-year-old me, the ten-year-old me? This is a dangerous path to go down. Building up your

resilience involves knowing your strengths and your deficiencies. Having identified your strengths, demonstrating behaviors that are in alignment with your strengths helps you develop those protective factors shown in the resiliency model. These strength-based behaviors will help you rebuff disruptions that will continue to come your way.

6. Immerse yourself in the visualization of positive fatherhood. After all, we all want to be the dad we never had right? It is therefore important that we are zeroed in on effective fatherhood as a goal of ours. With this goal in mind, you will be able to differentiate between those responses that help you elevate to being better fathers and those that can wound us or our children for years. Remind yourself of this goal daily. Father-centric art pieces in your home, inspiring pictures at work, reminders on your calendar, quotes about fatherhood, t-shirts with fatherhood slogans are all some basic mechanisms I have tried to immerse myself in positive fatherhood. Of course, these types of actions must be substantiated with other key aspects of fathering, some of which we cover in the remaining lessons.

Chapter 8 - Lesson #3
Best You, Not A Better Him

So far, you should have a draft of your Fatherhood Contract that describes the desired behaviors you would like to display as a parent. Even if you have not yet worked on your draft, at least you know that crafting one is an important reminder to you and your children of the type of father you wish to be. You should also understand the stressors associated with the experience of paternal absence or neglect, and how your adaptation to these stressors are crucial to your own growth and self-actualization. Learning how to hone resilient qualities and develop the habit of growing through adversity are important skills, given that our lives will most likely include continual disruptions. This leads us to our next lesson.

How many times have you said "I am going to be a better dad than I had" or "I will never do things like my dad" or "I am going to be so much better to my sons" or "I am going to create a new reality for my sons?" The lifelong lesson captured in this chapter is centered on your focus. Where is your energy focused? Putting this lesson into practice will require you to shift your mindset. It will challenge you to re-calibrate how you may have thought about things for years. And, if you never were afflicted with the mindset we are trying to change, then you have a head start on many of us who grew up with questions about the emotional presence of a loving father.

Over the years, when I spoke with fatherless men who became fathers themselves, I wanted to understand more about them. I had four fundamental intentions. First, I wanted to understand the attitudes, perceptions and beliefs of men who experienced father absence or father apathy. Second, I wanted to understand how experiences similar to mine had enabled or hampered men's ability to break generational trends of father absence in their families. Third, I wanted to identify the activities and competencies that assisted the development of fatherless men into models of effective fathering and positive male citizenship. Finally, I wanted to expand the body of knowledge about the issue. Research to date was primarily quantitative in nature, focused on making sweeping generalizations about fatherlessness as it related to things like crime, violence, cognitive impairment, social adaptation, academic performance, substance abuse, sexual promiscuity and relationship competence. I wanted to understand the issue in a deeper sense and embarked on a journey of capturing the true essence of the fatherless experience from those who lived it.

I must, however, admit that amidst all of those lofty intentions, I selfishly just wanted to understand the fatherless man better. I only had my viewpoint and I had lived with it for decades. So I wanted to know more! I sought to explore the common attitudes and approaches with others who shared my experience. As I learned more about the experience of others, I realized I was not alone. There were others who felt just as impacted, just as hurt, and just as confused and were just as concerned about the journey that was ahead. There were also many others who were equally motivated and inspired to make a difference for their children.

A major observation about the fatherless fathers I have met was their deep-rooted desire to provide a different father-son experience for their sons. Their intense resolve to be a more effective father was evident even if they had already in some way fallen short and replicated elements of their own fatherless experience with their offspring. These men had sheer pride in being a father, a desire to break the trend of fatherlessness, a drive to enable their sons to "tell a different story," a willingness to try alternative approaches to fathering, and belief in the mantra "imperfect but present" as factors contributing to their intense resolve to be more effective fathers.

This desire to create this different reality for their sons resulted in relentless comparison among the men I spoke with between the behaviors of their biological fathers and some of their own behaviors.

They were adamant that they were going to do better than their fathers in all aspects of their lives. One gentleman in particular with whom I conversed spoke of his disdain for his biological father's involvement in gang activity. When prompted about some of his lifestyle choices that may have been influenced by his absent father, the young man described his reservations about how effective his father was as a gang member and questioned whether his father was even good at being a respected "gang banger." Additionally, the young man made it clear that he too was a gang member. Although his affiliation with gangs was inspired by his father, he emphasized that he out-performed his father as a committed gang member.

This conversation sparked a realization in me. As fatherless men committed to creating a difference in our families, we often tend to use the dysfunctional behaviors of our fathers as the reference point against which we evaluate our own behavior. We become so focused on out-doing our fathers and not "doing what they did" that we lose sight of our own potential. We cease setting our own behavioral goals and even learn to be satisfied with our outcomes…as long as they are better than those of our fathers. I mean, the pride that the young man I spoke of displayed at having surpassed his father's performance as a gang affiliate was profound. Even in negativity, he tried his utmost to do better than his father, illustrating his own blindness to what he could achieve had he simply focused on his own potential, competence and excellence.

I am reminded of another experience that further confirmed this realization for me. A few years ago, I fell in love with the idea of riding a motorcycle. I spent a significant amount of time learning more and more about motorcycles—the different types, the engine sizes, the various manufacturers, ratings and reviews, etc. I watched with envy as motorcyclists zoomed by and thought about the freedom they must experience while riding. I listened with pleasure at the roar of the engines when I pulled up next to them in traffic and giggled like a kid at the riders who used "highway bars" to allow them to sprawl their legs while on long rides.

I decided to take the plunge and get my own bike but I wanted to do everything "the right way." So, I signed up for motorcycle safety school. It included several hours of guided classroom study and a three-day practicum during which we actually learned to ride safely. I marveled during the class at the instructors who were able to move people who had never ridden a motorcycle before to confidently riding on the training circuit in a rather short timeframe.

One activity required student riders to navigate through a course littered with several cones. The exercise was a solid evaluation of riding skills but really tested one's concentration and focus. My first time through the cones, I was hesitant and nervous. Those 12-inch orange cones towered like skyscrapers against the black asphalt. They seemed so close together! How could I get this motorcycle to move through these obstacles at a pace that was slow enough to prevent me from over-running my turns and fast enough to prevent me from spilling. Needless to say, I had a somewhat dramatic fall on my first run. It occurred as I was riding at approximately 10 miles per hour, so my ego was more hurt than I was physically. An instructor rushed over to my assistance to coach me through my mistakes and to send me back around to get it right.

I learned a couple things from this experience. First of all, my fall at 10 mph was all I needed to convince me that a fall at 50, 60, 70 mph would not be a pleasant experience. But my most important lesson was embedded in the conversation that ensued between the coach and me.

"Are you ok?" The coach yelled as he ran over to my bike.

"I'm fine. I thought I had it," I responded, with what I knew was an embarrassed look on my face. I thought I knew what I had done wrong but the coach was insistent that we needed to chat about it.

"Let's talk about this. What do you think went wrong there?"

"Well, I thought I had good speed as I entered the cones and was going fine until the sharp turn."

The riding coach continued. "Ok, I was watching you closely. Your approach was good although I could tell that you weren't riding confidently. You were hesitant. I was also watching your eyes trying to determine where your focus was as you entered the cones. What were you looking at?"

"I was making sure that I stayed away from the cones," I muttered, my confidence clearly waning.

"I know!" the coach snapped back. "But here is the deal. Believe it or not, this big motorcycle does not have a mind of its own.

It will only go where you guide it. And the way you guide it is to focus on where you want it to go. Your head and eyes should be directed to where you want the bike to go and it will go there! Get back in line and try it!"

"What do you mean?" I asked sheepishly.

The coach put his hand on my shoulder and said "Listen, you cannot focus on the cones. You must look into the spaces where you want this motorcycle to go. Your head and eyes are very important in guiding the bike. If you look at the obstacles, guess where you are going? If you look and focus on the spaces between the obstacles, where do you think the motorcycle will go?"

"Really?"

"Get back in line and try it" the coach said as he helped me lift my training school bike off the ground.

I refocused and circled around to navigate the obstacle course again. As I approached, I reminded myself of the coach's advice. I completely blocked out the cones and focused on the path between them. Focusing on the path around the obstacles helped me to better monitor my speed, my lean in the curves, and where I positioned the bike in anticipation of the next turn. It worked! I emerged from the obstacle course and gave a complimentary roar of the engine to show my appreciation to my riding coach. I saw him in my periphery giving me a thumbs up and a slow methodical applause.

That day, I navigated the obstacles with ease five more times and completed the training course successfully. I went on to purchase my own cruiser. The words of the riding coach at the motorcycle school echoed in my mind every time I sat on Goliath! Yes, picture it! A modern day picture of David and Goliath! Goliath was the moniker that I bestowed on my bike—a cruiser with a beautiful custom-painted body that featured purple with dark purple flames, polished leather seats, and perfectly formed saddle bags. Everything else on Goliath was Chrome. He had custom pipes that made him roar, while providing sufficient noise that gave us quite the presence on the road. Needless to say, David and Goliath spent countless hours together…just bonding. These hours helped me hone my motorcycling skills but also provided me with moments of peaceful reflection. As I reflected, the more I realized that the things you learn on a bike are applicable to daily life experiences. Motorcycling proved to be a great metaphor for life.

"Don't focus on the cones! Look where you want to go! Look, Lean, Press and Roll."

That was the guidance yelled out by the riding coaches at the motorcycling safety school. The steps of look, lean, press and roll were the steps used for making a turn with a motorcycle. First and foremost, the rider must *look* by shifting his head, pointing his eyes into the curve. Next, he must *lean* the motorcycle into the corner, *press* on the handle bar and *roll* on the throttle to safely pick up speed in the corner. The bike, as they taught at the school, always follows wherever the rider's eyes go. If you are correctly focused on your path

89

around the bend and between any obstacles, that is where the bike will go. Similarly, if you are looking at the obstacles or at the pavement…you get the picture!

How does this relate to life? Specifically, what does it mean for those of us who experienced fatherlessness and are stuck trying to be better than our biological dads? Think about it. When I was making my first run through the obstacles at the motorcycle school, I was consumed with looking at the obstacles, determined not to hit them. Isn't that the very thing we do when we build our lives focused on not being like our fathers? Are we not focused on "the obstacles?" Imagine the asphalt area littered with those bright orange cones. The cones metaphorically represent all of those characteristics of our fathers that we intensely focus on "bettering." We get so caught up in wanting to be more present than, more loving than, more connected than, more considerate than, more tolerant than, more involved than, more of a teacher than our fathers. Our attention is squarely placed on the obstacles.

What is also more devastating in this lesson is what happens when we are focused on the obstacles in our lives. From my example, you focus on the obstacles you are trying to avoid and you hit them! That does not bode well for those of us who are really determined to avoid being like our fathers. Some of us will invariably hit that very thing that we are focused on avoiding. This is huge! It suggests to us that we have to pay more attention to where we place our energy. I have personally seen how my determination to be better than my father guided me to demonstrate some of the very behaviors I detested in him.

So why would we continue to build our lives in relation to something we do not wish to become? We need to place more emphasis on navigating the fatherless life experience by focusing on the path between all the resultant obstacles that are presented to us— concentrating on the path among the cones and not on the cones themselves. In other words, you, my friend must challenge yourself to be the best you and let go of trying to be a better him. No longer should you satisfy yourself with performance related to fatherhood simply because you did better than your father. The key question is did you do it to the best of your ability? Establishing the bar at your absent father's performance could very well constitute selling yourself short and setting goals that are not even challenging enough. The best YOU…not a better HIM!

Chapter 9 - Lesson #4
Teach! Teach! Teach!

We have placed a lot of emphasis on the importance of fathers as models of positive male citizenship. We have established that they are instrumental in contributing to the emotional, social and cognitive development of their children. Traditionally, father roles have centered on being a financial provider and family protector. Fatherless men I spoke with identified several roles that men play but singled out a few that were more important to them as a result of their life experience.

Gone are the days when you could leave home in the wee hours of the morning, head off to work a 12-14 hour day, return after your kids' bedtime, read the newspaper, go to bed and repeat this the following day. The times are long gone when it was assumed that all you had to do to be considered a good father was to earn money. You can no longer earn the respect of being an outstanding father if you are emotionally disconnected. There are greater demands placed on your ability to serve as a guide, teacher and source of validation for your children.

This lesson is about honing the contributions you make in your children's lives. How would you like your sons/daughters to remember the role you played in their childhood? These guidelines may already be obvious to you. However, I wanted to share what I deciphered as ways in which we can strengthen our father-child bonds, while satisfying what several fatherless men indicate was their most important need that went unmet. The needs they described may not necessarily be what one may expect but they definitely intrigued me as I learned more about their experiences.

One common need that our children, especially our sons, share is for us to be sources of affirmation. I had a lengthy conversation with one fatherless man whose name was Jeban. When I spoke with Jeban, he described a remarkable analogy that highlighted his thoughts on the need for a father's validation.

"We take pictures for moments. As we go through life, we take mental pictures of moments and if fathers are not there for those moments, there is a key component missing. When I did well, I wanted desperately to hear my father say 'that was good, son.'"

Another man, Dave, concurred and was adamant that, based on his experiences, the single most important way in which a father could satisfy the needs of his growing child was validating them. As a devout Christian man, Dave also provided a powerful story that cemented for him what he needed to do as a father.

> "Let me say it this way. I believe in God…and I got a revelation one day. When Jesus was baptized…and he rose from the water and then the heavens opened up, and then the spirit of God came down in the form of a dove. And God's own voice says, 'This is my beloved son, in whom I'm well pleased.' And I read that and read that, just thinking…Oh…God's telling the people watching Jesus be baptized, 'Listen to my son, because he's my son.' And my thought was, so what is God doing? He's validating Jesus, right? You're MY baby boy. I'm proud of YOU. And my thought was, if Jesus, a perfect man, needed to be validated by his father, then how much do our imperfect children need the same validation?"

Regardless of your religious persuasion, this is a powerful story that emphasizes the confidence-building role that an affirming and validating father can play in the life of a child.

Although being a source of validation is highly important, it was not the most popular response when men were prompted to provide the most valuable role a father plays. The most prominent response was the need for fathers to be teachers to their children and more specifically, models to their sons. This sounds simple enough, right? Isn't this obvious? Well, what was most fascinating about this, in my view, was the fact that these men who grew up with this void in their lives were able to identify the very thing they believed would have made a significant difference in their lives. They pointed to a role that they never had as one that was most important. So let us look at all the ways you can model or teach as you continue on your quest to be an amazing dad.

1. Model what being a man means. As a father, you must be sold on teaching your sons the fundamental aspects of being a man. Similarly, you must be as equally bought in to teaching your daughters how a man should behave toward them. We may acknowledge that our mothers were rather capable at relaying some lessons on certain aspects of manhood. Several men who grew up longing for the involved guidance of their fathers indicated that these teachings would have been more "digestible" if they came from their dads. What does that mean? It means that you must remain on the lookout for those lessons that may have more credibility and meaning when taught by a father. Make them a part of your contract from Lesson #1. Some examples include developmental experiences, ranging from simple things like sports, tying a tie, shaving, and how to give a meaningful handshake to more significant things like dealing with relationships. Granted, many readers may suggest that a woman can teach these things just fine! To which I respond "True!" However, based on my experience and my conversations with

fatherless men, it seems as though lessons would have meant more coming from our fathers.

2. Teach From Your Experience. In my contract to my sons, Item 9 and 10 stated, "I will be candid with you about my mistakes in life so that you can avoid the pitfalls that I fell into" and "I will reveal to you, in a non-boastful manner, the characteristics that I have that helped me overcome many challenges and achieve a level of success." As a current father or aspiring dad, it is imperative that you guide your children by drawing on your own experiences. Understanding where you made missteps and where you made great choices are instrumental nuggets that help your children navigate the transition from childhood to preteen to adolescence to adulthood. One of the men I spoke with over the years mastered this. He practiced this experiential transparency to gain the trust of his son so effectively that he challenged his sons to describe a scenario that they could possibly endure but that he had not.

    "Name one scenario that you've been through that I haven't been through yet," he would say to his sons. "Furthermore, don't be afraid to talk to me about anything, because I'm not going to tell you what to do, but I'll tell you how it affected me, how I made wrong decisions, so that you can make the right one!"

3. Teach effective behaviors for family life. Your children will learn from you how to operate in a family setting. Now this may be difficult for you, particularly since you may not have had the same guidance throughout your own transition into manhood.

Therefore, there is significant chance that you will do some trial and error in this space. I know that I definitely fell short in my understanding of how a man/father operates in the context of a family. Over time I have realized a couple things I believe you may find helpful in your family.

- Be perseverant and relentless in promoting family unity. Your children should know, based on your actions, that the togetherness of the family is your number one priority.

- Be cognizant of your shortcomings and seek professional guidance. Model candor and acknowledgment of flaws. Your children will benefit from exposure to your humanness and learn from the steps you take to supplement your flaws, and operate effectively in your strengths.

- Be connected emotionally. Although this will be covered as its own lesson a few chapters ahead, this is so important for the family unity that I thought I should mention it here. While this may be unnatural, doing whatever it takes to be in tune with your emotionality and showing your children that it is ok to do so will go a long way.

With the discussion on important roles fathers play and the differentiated outcomes of the fatherless experience, there is an interesting side effect that I observed in myself. It was later confirmed as a legitimate side effect of father absence through my conversations with others who shared my experience.

I pondered for many years how to characterize my response to what occurred between my father and me. As I reflect, I realize that after the break-up of my family, when my mother, my brother and I were separated from my father, I became what I refer to as an achievement junkie. I focused on adding structure and discipline in my life as substitutes for what I thought was missing. I did this by joining a paramilitary youth organization that focused on teaching young teens aspects of leadership, community involvement and civic responsibility. To do this, the organization leveraged lessons in military science and leadership. In addition, I became obsessed with achievement. My level of competitiveness and drive to achieve was out of control. This lasted from my teenage years and I think it still is an influential aspect of my life even to this day. But what is at the root of this achievement junkie complex? I only recently sat down to get to the root of this sometimes approach to life that on the surface parades as ambition but can be quite unhealthy.

What I discovered was that I faced a situation in which I never had the comforting words of a father who said "Son, well done!" I therefore spent all my life going after achievement, hoping to achieve a level of performance that would merit these affirming words from my father. Of course, I had no relationship with my dad after the split, so even if he wanted to say such encouraging words to me, it was impossible. As I thought more about this situation, I began to describe it as "living in an un-calibrated state"—never knowing what "well done" looked like. Imagine the stress associated with chasing something that is undefined.

I later learned that I was not alone in this. Numerous dads have faced the same issue. It is incumbent upon you to ensure that you provide your children with the progress reminders to preclude them living their lives in an "un-calibrated state." Remember, to be that dad you never had, you are going to have to be comfortable being the source of affirmation and being an effective teacher for your children. Now that we have this dialed in, let's move to the next lesson—Presence over perfection.

Chapter 10 - Lesson #5
Presence over Perfection

Of all of the lessons unveiled so far, I believe this one is a crucial, foundational one. In my exploration of the fatherhood and fatherlessness phenomenon, I recognized that there are often several factors that contribute to the physical or emotional separation between a father and his children. Let's revisit our working definition of fatherlessness one more time.

> "Fatherlessness is a combination of physical and emotional distance between fathers and children that results from a continuum of paternal behaviors ranging from apathy to outright abandonment."

Recall that the highlight of this definition is the implication that emotional disconnection originating from paternal apathy can lead to a physically present father somehow having fatherless children. This is often a hard pill to swallow for some fathers who may still subscribe to the belief that if they are a solid financial support for their families, then they have done their part. Of course, the whole premise of this book is that both your emotional and physical presence are necessary for you to be that dad who makes a difference for future generations.

Without reservation, I always held the belief that it was incomprehensible how fathers could live their lives void of a relationship with their children. However, after I became a father myself and had engaged in conversation with many who shared the fatherless experience, I came to the realization that committed fatherhood, like motherhood, is extremely hard. Like any other relationship, the father-child interaction requires work, dedication, time, tolerance, care and mutual respect. Though difficult, fatherhood can be a thoroughly rewarding experience for some, but can also be a difficult wake-up call for others. Some men enter fatherhood enamored by the excitement of holding a newborn or the prospect of attending a high school or college graduation. They somehow fail to acknowledge that there are approximately 11,000,000 minutes between these two events—each of which is an opportunity to bolster or wound your young one.

In my attempt to break this issue up into little manageable chunks, I often thought of what would be an impetus for men to physically or emotionally disconnect from their children. After hours of reflection and internal and external conversations, I came to the conclusion that many men experience pressure that demands they perform at a certain level. An inability to perform at this societally enforced level constitutes nothing short of failure for many and is a source of embarrassment for some. So what is this pressure and where does it come from?

I found a plausible answer to this question in the study of masculinity and its linkages to fatherhood. By now, it should be clear to us that in the face of a lack of modelling from an emotionally and socially absent father, we are often left to derive our view of masculinity from the media, work environments, society, and any other power relationships in which we are involved. As you may attest, these sources of "masculinity training" are seldom unbiased. It is no secret that some of these sources may enforce some traditional views of masculinity that are limiting in emotionality and skewed as far as how men operate in our relationships with women and even with other men. So let us briefly uncover how some of these historical elements combined with the fatherless man's search for masculinity lessons in all the wrong places could contribute to our ineffective paternal practices.

Perceptions about masculinity and linked elements of fatherhood have been in flux throughout history. In the early 1980s, there was an idea floating around in the research world that men had very specific societal roles. This belief, it was soon found, did not explain why there was such differentiated power among men. It did not explain why some men were significantly more dominant over others. I mean, shouldn't the power among men be equivalent if it were solely based on the role they played in society?

Further research into various cultures uncovered the assertion that there were indeed numerous forms of masculinity and that there were even multiple tiers of masculinity. Moreover, all these tiers of masculinity were dominated by a single type described as "the hegemon." By definition, the hegemon was distinguished from all other forms of masculinity and could only be enacted by very few men. It described, in rather rigid terms, the most honored way of being a man as a repression of anything perceived as effeminate in men and implied that all men positioned themselves in relation to "the hegemon."

I read widely about this and wanted to conduct my own mini-experiment. So, I went online and I conducted an image search for the term "hegemonic masculinity." I was pretty intrigued at the results. At the time I conducted this search, the number one image returned was that of the Marlboro man. Why was that? With the blitz of tobacco advertising that took place in the 1970s, the image of the Marlboro man illustrated below became synonymous with various characteristics desired in a "man."

He was strong, physically fit and quite chiseled. He had neatly cropped brown hair and deep blue eyes. He was tall and oozed virility. His demeanor was serious and focused, with little evidence that he would be emotionally expressive. He was the quintessential cowboy who had conquered his surroundings having braved the West. He tamed his beasts—the wildest of horses—and did it all with ease. He used his enviable skills to round up thousand-pound bulls—he conquered those too. Other images of the Marlboro Man suggested he also had complete control over his consumption of substances. Alcohol and tobacco usage were an everyday thing that was done effortlessly and with very little impact on his presence. Moreover, he was invincible, not subject to the negative impacts of these substances, despite the Surgeon General's warning that normally accompanied his image. Through other imagery, I could deduce that he was also great with the ladies, as he was often illustrated as very comfortable in the presence of multiple women, none of whom seemed bothered that they were one of many.

I know what you are thinking! So what? What does hegemonic masculinity have to do with being a fatherless father? Well, imagine the implications if this representation of masculinity was the accepted description of how men should behave and exist in the context of our society. Furthermore, since all men, by definition, strive to reach this "hegemonic" existence with very few ever reaching it, think about the struggle and internal conflict as men endured futile attempts to mimic the legendary Marlboro Man. To bring this closer to home, think about the disconnection from any form of emotionality—considered feminine—and how this played into your own experience of fatherlessness. How does this serve as a threat to you fulfilling your desire to be a dad with a difference?

The struggle that ensues as we attempt to be like the Marlboro Man can be destructive. Subsequent research concluded that the pursuit of patriarchal power hampers emotional expression among men and depicts real men as those who do not feel pain, cry or reveal fear—myths that can lead to inadequacy and anger. The inevitable failure to meet all that the media portrays as "the hegemon" can crush our spirits as men and cause us to begin doubting our abilities. The self-doubt associated with "falling short" reminds me of something that I once read in the 2001 John Eldredge book *Wild at Heart*. The author alluded to the fact that men face numerous identity challenges with the fundamental question at the forefront of their manhood being "Do I have what it takes?" This question is applicable in multiple settings:

"Do I have what it takes as a great _____ (fill in the occupation)?"

"Do I have what it takes as a boyfriend?"

"Do I have what it takes as a husband?"

"Do I have what it takes as a lover?"

"Do I have what it takes as a friend?"

"Do I have what it takes as an employee?"

"Do I have what it takes as an entrepreneur?"

"Do I have what it takes as an athlete?"

"Do I have what it takes as a coach?"

"Do I have what it takes as a teacher?"

"Do I have what it takes as a student?"

"Do I have what it takes as an author?"

"Do I have what it takes as a MAN?"

"Do I have what it takes as a SON?"

"Do I have what it takes as a FATHER?"

I believe that these questions are on our minds when we adapt to new roles or strive to be better in the roles we already have. I know, for sure, that I questioned whether I was good enough, tall enough, strong enough, fast enough, handsome enough, smart enough, disciplined enough, or savvy enough to do many of the things I have attempted. What about you? Have you questioned yourself? When was the last time you did? What was the outcome?

The tension between this media-driven, societally enforced form of masculinity and emotionally connected fatherhood has and continues to be a source of struggle for men. We are constantly challenged to maintain an emotionally driven paternal involvement that conflicts with many of the traditional characterizations of manhood to which we were exposed. How can we strive to be like what is societally accepted—a lack of emotional expression and softness—and still live out the loving emotionally tolerant, nurturing fathers we are also told we should become. This conflict can be a major source of turmoil for many of us.

The media and societal norms have somehow convinced some of us that the pursuit of this hegemon is synonymous with the pursuit of perfection. This simply sets us up for disappointment when we consider our naturally self-doubting, do-I-have-what-it-takes mindset. Let's say we go through an episode during which we bombard ourselves with these questions. What if you somehow convinced yourself that the answer was "No?" What behaviors do you think you would rationalize as a result of the disappointment that follows?

While we are busy pursuing the unreachable in some cases, what are our children requiring of us as fathers? When I asked men who grew up with the void of a father, none of them ever mentioned they wanted perfection. Instead, they mentioned the simple things like having someone to talk to, someone who was present for milestone moments, someone who could provide a blueprint of what to do, or someone to assist with making life-changing decisions. Some of the men I spoke to were star athletes, reaching junior Olympic status and performing exceptionally even at the collegiate level. Despite their amazing performances, some of which still grace the record books at schools across the nation, they mentioned one common source of disappointment.

"I would look at everybody else on my team and those I was competing against and they would have their fathers. Then I would look in the stands and I would see nobody. I wonder what my life would be like if my father was there," one man said. Another stated, "I really felt like I needed him to help me with how to interact with my peers, particularly in sports." Yet another recalled a heart-wrenching story. He was a junior in high school when his football team played for the state championship. As one of the star players on the team, he reached out to his absentee father who committed to being present. Although he was by now accustomed to his father's absence, this was the most important game of his football career to date and he longed for his father to witness it.

"I looked up in the stands. Again, he was not there. But, he told me he was going to be here! I was empty!" Almost tearfully, this young man continued to share this story to me almost 20 years after it occurred. "Even though my mother was there, even though many family members came from everywhere to watch the game, he was not there! I kept looking up to the stands, and I remember crying at halftime. We ended up losing that game but the pain of losing pales in comparison to the disappointment I felt when he did not show up for me."

As men who endured fatherlessness, we are all too familiar with that pain. It may not be a sporting event. It may be a graduation or a recital or just a moment at the kitchen table as you poured over information packets from colleges trying to chart your future. It might have been a moment when simply knowing you had his emotional backing would have been sufficient.

One such experience that was etched in my memory occurred when I was ten years old. Back then, our educational system in Barbados used a national examination at age 10-11 to determine which secondary school you would attend. I was a pretty academically gifted kid but I also worked tirelessly in preparation for this examination. The day of the exam came and went. The nervousness was high but I was confident that I would do well. When all the dust had settled, I was notified that I had achieved the highest grade of all the boys in the nation.

"You mean in the whole country?" I remember asking my mother.

"Yes. You did very well!"

The flurry of attention that followed was pretty enjoyable at that age. A journalist and photographer from our national newspaper visited my home to interview me. My picture and interview covered the entire back page of the newspaper. My mother and extended family were elated. However, my father never said a word to me about it. It was only in one of his moments of drunkenness that he said the following words to me that I am soundly convinced broke me that day. After bringing up the fact that my story was in the newspaper, he yelled,

"So you think you are a f&*%# celebrity? You think you are special?"

I was in shock. I relive that moment frequently. In the midst of my 10-year-old moment of celebration, my father did not have it in him to even feel proud. I am your son, am I not? Shouldn't you be reveling in this moment as well? Shouldn't you be overcome with pride that YOUR SON accomplished this? All I wanted at that moment was for him to be emotionally present for me. For him to show up and, as the previous chapter suggests, just say "Well done, Son!" I did not need perfection from him, just his presence.

While your circumstances may be different, I believe that a key to overcoming the fatherless experience and moving beyond it is the recognition of how important the little things are and how unimportant and actually unrealistic perfection is. This realization is not easy for me to grasp because of my self-admitted achievement junkie outlook; hence, I carved it into my contract so I am constantly reminded of it. Remember in my contract where I said I will be candid about my flaws? This was my way of telling my boys I will strive to be present, flaws and all.

So, as you move forward, please recognize that you can turn the mistakes you make or have made into valuable lessons for both you and your children. Own them! Commit to trying your utmost not to make the same mistakes twice! And show up physically, emotionally and socially each time you have an opportunity. Your perfection is not required but your presence is certainly desired!

Chapter 11 - Lesson #6
Embrace the Emotional Man

Nature or Nurture? This is a question that has been asked for decades about many behavioral patterns among men and women. There are several expectations society has placed on both sexes as they relate to their behavior. As I mentioned before, the root of many of the challenges men face is the relentless pursuit of patriarchal power coupled with the rejection of uninhibited emotional expression. Men are somehow taught or influenced by their surroundings to believe that real men are those who do not feel pain, acknowledge pain, cry, reveal fear or expose their own vulnerabilities in anyway.

Even with all of the elements in place for a functional, adaptive upbringing, some of the societal norms for masculine behaviors are in my view, myths that can lead to anger, feelings of inadequacy and frustration. There is significant pressure imposed by society's expectations to conform to limited emotionality regardless of family structure, economic situation or other socio-economic factors.

The fatherless men I spoke with over the years consistently expressed the belief that their emotional wellbeing was hampered by their life experiences associated with flawed paternal interaction. They perceived that the deficiencies in their own emotional development affected the transition into manhood and were key contributors in shaping the men they became. Many factors may have contributed to the challenges with emotionality. However, it is no coincidence that these men attribute much of this to their lack of a paternal influence. One man said "…absolutely my father's absence had an impact. And so did my environment. Where I grew up, if you cry, you are a punk! If you hugged, you are a punk! That was a show of weakness!"

Another young man quipped dismissively about emotional expression, "Not allowed. Without having a father like a lot of people I knew in that environment, it was not the norm to cry. Suck it up! Don't cry!"

One gentleman went as far as to describe his belief that his sons should never see him expressing emotions that may be considered soft. "That would probably never happen! I have to be the pillar of my family, the strong one, the rock!"

In one memorable conversation with a middle aged man who grew up from age four without his father, he mentioned that in the absence of his father during his adolescent years, he received some advice from other adults who ushered him "to grow a spine" and "to never let anyone see him as weak." That advice, though well intentioned, haunted him for many years. He described the impact of that advice. "I kept everything bottled up, and I didn't show any emotions. Because my perception of manliness was strength—one who never lets his family see him weak."

Another man, a 33-year-old father of two who had himself missed out on a healthy relationship with his dad described himself as emotionless and cold. He stated, "When dealing with certain situations, it is like I have a black heart, like there is ice in my veins. I am really trying to add emotional expression as part of who I am, but that is just what I learned from my father—never let your emotions out like that."

These conversations highlighted that the lack of an effective model as it relates to emotionality can be disruptive to the emotional wellbeing of a young man. The myths about manliness and the avoidance of a show of emotions communicated by society and by the environments of desensitization in which fatherlessness thrives can have lifelong impact.

Can you relate to the experiences they shared? Have you ever been told the three most devastating words that any growing young man can hear, "Be a man!"? For those of us who have, it is an unfortunate experience that wounds us for a long time.

Another factor that comes into play when we consider the emotional development of fatherless men, is the fact that many of us, as a result of our fathers' physical or emotional absence, are thrust into adult-like roles rather early. With the added pressure of fulfilling the responsibilities of a missing father figure in the home, we tend to harden ourselves emotionally. We turn to "toughing up" as a means of coping with the pressure of growing up fast and making adult decisions during adolescence. We limit the gamut of emotions we are able to put on display.

The struggle with displaying emotion is by no means an indication that we don't have feelings at any given moment. On the contrary, there are several emotions we simply bottle up inside. They are felt but not shown. Examples include feelings of fear, skepticism, mistrust, disrespect, inadequacy and emasculation. Many of those with whom I conversed about the fatherless experience acknowledge being driven by fear. They cited the fear of failing as a father, fear of repeating wounding behaviors, fear of passing on negative generational habits, fear of not knowing how to father and fear of not being good enough. The feeling of fear of failure went beyond the role of father and into apprehension about their situational awareness and their ability to deal with the scenarios they faced when they entered adulthood.

I remember talking to my older son once about some decisions I made regarding his privileges and a tough stance I was taking with regard to aspects of his behavior. In explaining my decisions, I said to him, "Son, I know that I am strict with you!" As he contemplated the situation, he interrupted me, "Dad, that's what fathers do!" I remember how much his words struck me. I nodded toward him as if I was saying "yes, that's what they do! And I do it from a place of love." But deep down inside, I questioned whether I really even had a clue what fathers really did.

My confidence as a father waivers as I sometimes confront feelings of inadequacy. The feelings of inadequacy and apprehensiveness I felt were well represented by one gentlemen who said to me, "there was just too much pressure that I placed on myself. And like they say, pressure busts a pipe, and that is what happened. When my pipe burst, I reverted to negative behaviors that ultimately took me out of the fathering situation, away from my kids and away from that kind of pressure."

Despite the swirling emotions trapped inside, we live as though we are not allowed or it is in some way unmanly to be emotionally honest and expressive. Instead, we choose to internalize pain, deal with it on our own and allow feelings to build up and fester. No wonder we feel misunderstood! We cannot, regardless of how hard we try, become effective men or fathers when we start from such a place of emotional deficit. It is akin to starting a race 10 yards behind the other competitors, or wearing a 50-pound vest for a race you have been preparing for all your life. We literally carry an unnecessary burden when we choose to reject our own emotionality.

Related to the struggles with displaying emotion is the tolerance of emotional expression in others. Because we may live by the rules of minimal emotionality, we tend to transfer this requirement to others. Unfortunately, our children, especially our sons, typically bear the brunt of our false sense of bravado. According to the Conflict of Learned Behaviors, we have some natural behaviors, based on our own socialization that may conflict with more accepted behaviors we acquire. This conflict is on display when we deal with emotional expression in others. Let me share a story to illustrate this.

When my sons were younger, I had many of the fears about my own preparedness to teach, guide, influence, nurture and be the dad I didn't have. I realized rather early on that I had a natural discomfort with my boys crying. I later found out that many fathers, whether they were fatherless or not, shared a similar discomfort. The burden society places on us with respect to our expression of sadness or disappointment is real. Nevertheless, my own maturity level when I became a parent, coupled with the fact that I had chosen a path of constant personal development informed my mindset that emotional expression was a crucial part of growing up. I knew I had to work hard at ensuring that I honored this when dealing with my sons.

When I noticed how uncomfortable I was with my sons' crying, I quickly devised my own tactical response. In the early stages of implementing my response, here is how a typical scenario

117

would unfold. I would be sitting in my office or bedroom reading. I could hear the rumble and unbridled laughter emerging from another room as my sons wrestled or roughhoused with each other. I would plead with them to calm down but to no avail. Invariably, a scream would pierce the air as one of the boys always ended up crying. Hearing the scream, I knew I had to go check on them but I learned to pause and have a conversation with myself to devise a game plan.

"Now David," I whispered, "when you enter this room, you know you will encounter one or both of your sons in tears. Breathe. Make sure they are safe. Find out who is hurt. Get to eye level with the crier and let him know it is going to be ok. Hug him. Relax. Now—Ready—BREAK!"

With my quick tactical plan in place, I would enter the room ready to handle the situation. As I entered, I would first quickly ensure no one was truly hurt and despite my plan of action, what happened next would always throw me off.

I would open my mouth and this is what was blurted out. "What is going on in here? Why are you crying? You need to go to your room, calm down and then come talk to me!"

My natural behavior, based on what I had seen over the years, was "winning." But that spelled victory for no one. My boys did not benefit from that and neither did I. I quickly retrained myself to overcome that natural reaction and used it to fuel my pursuit of being a better father. I focus on seeing beyond the emotional expression— the crying—and place greater emphasis on what triggered the crying itself. The growth that I realized, once I pinpointed how my natural behaviors affected my sons and chose to do something about it was invaluable. Here are some guidelines I assembled in order to help you with embracing the emotional man.

1. Recognize when/if there is a problem. Reflect on the times when you had intense feelings about an issue and chose not to share those feelings with anyone. Consider the pressure you placed yourself under. Identify the circumstances under which you felt more inclined to "keep stuff bottled up."

2. Be aware of how that pent up emotion from #1 impacts the people around you that you care about (e.g., spouse, partner, children, other family members, friends, coworkers, etc.) Is it manifesting itself as agitation, frustration, or even anger?

3. Unpack your "relationship with emotional expression." What are the mindsets that were instilled in you that form your viewpoints on emotionality? Who/what influenced you to be constrained in how you expressed emotion? What do others say about how emotionally expressive you are?

4. The items in 1-3 are personal and require you to be rather candid with yourself about how you deal with emotions. This recommendation may be a little tougher to swallow. I recommend that you seek out the help of a professional counselor or coach to help with emotional expression. They are prepared to guide you through the thought process that gets you to the root issues as well as to help you understand why your own emotional honesty is crucial in your important relationships.

5. Invest in yourself by further developing your communication skills. Emotions are rather tricky entities. They can cause you to communicate poorly or not at all, as we have discovered. Learning how to have impactful conversations even when under duress is an important skill of a father who embraces emotionality in others. So, what constitutes effective communication? It is less about exchanging words and more about comprehending the emotions and purpose that are behind the information being shared. The art of effective communication enables you to share a message and have it received exactly as you intended. To do this, several skills are required—attentive listening, nonverbal cues, stress management, confidence in communicating, understanding your own emotions, and recognizing the emotions of those with whom you are communicating. Your success at honing your communication is the glue that will help you deepen your connection with your family, your children and others while improving your effectiveness at decision making and problem solving. As a father, you will, on numerous occasions, have to deliver difficult messages and a focus on improving in this area will help you communicate these difficult messages without creating more conflict or destroying the trust in your father-child relationships.

6. Discover the power of an "I" message. The term "I message" was coined by Thomas Gordon in the 1960s. Using an "I message" when sharing emotions keeps the focus on how you are feeling as opposed to who was responsible or what someone else

did. It is an assertion about what you are feeling and contrasts with a "you statement," which is about the person you are speaking with. Not using an "I" message approach when sharing your feelings may often trigger defensiveness in those around you. Your goal in talking openly about your emotions should be to put others at ease while communicating how you feel. Here is an example of the recipe for a powerful "I" message. It may feel a little weird the first few times you use it but with practice it becomes a go-to tool in your fatherhood toolkit.

The "I" Message

I feel [INSERT EMOTION/FEELING WORD] when [DESCRIBE WHAT CAUSED THE FEELING]. I would like [DESCRIBE WHAT YOU WANT TO HAPPEN INSTEAD].

Let's say your son brought home a note from his teacher describing some negative classroom behavior that he has been demonstrating of late. When you get together to chat with him, your "I statement" could possibly look like this:

> *I feel **DISAPPOINTED** and **EMBARRASSED** when **YOUR BEHAVIOR IN THE CLASSROOM IS NOT WHAT IT SHOULD BE**. I would like **YOU TO BE MORE AWARE AND CONSIDERATE OF YOUR CLASSMATES**.*

The emotion or feeling word must precede any description of what causes you to feel the way you do. Examples of feeling words include: sad, happy, frustrated, concerned, confused, depressed, encouraged, appreciated, worried, unheard, unwanted and grateful.

The "I" Message PLUS

One of the key advantages of the "I" message is that it enables effective expression of emotion. However, one of the challenges it creates is that the person with whom you are communicating may become defensive. You can take certain steps to upgrade the effectiveness of your "I" message. One is active listening. As an active listener, you paraphrase and reflect back what the other person is saying in response to your "I" message. Here is a side-by-side example of an effective combination of the "I" message and active listening versus an ineffective one. In both scenarios, a father is conversing with one of his children. He is concerned about the child's failure to inform his parents of his whereabouts and uses the following "I message":

Father: Son, I feel frustrated when you don't let us know where you are

Son: And? Well isn't that too bad?

The child here has responded in a rather rude manner to the dad. Look at these two different responses:

Scenario #1	Scenario #2
Father: You feel angry when I tell you how I am feeling angry.	Father: Who do you think you are talking to me with that tone, young man? Go to your room right now!
Son: You're right! You don't care how I'm feeling, so why should I care about how YOU are feeling?	Son: No! I am not going to my room! Make me!
Father: You feel unsure about whether or not I care about your feelings.	Father: That's enough! You are losing all privileges for a month!
Son: You don't care about anybody.	Son: Sure! Who cares? I'm tired of living here anyway! Good-bye!
Father: You feel disappointed that I don't seem to care about anybody.	
Son: Actually, I know that you care about me. I just hate you hovering over me all the time.	
Father: You feel resentful that I pay attention to what you are doing.	
Son: Yes, I think that you don't trust me.	

Father: You are afraid that I
don't trust you.

Son: Yes that is how it seems
when you are always asking
me where I am going or
what I am doing.

Father: You feel insulted when I
ask about your plans,
because that suggests that I
don't trust you to make the
right decision.

Son: That's right and I hate it.

Father: You feel pretty angry
that I don't trust you to
make the right decision.

Son: Oh, I know that you trust
me, but I am a little older
now and I want some space
to live my own life.

Father: You feel sure that you
are capable of making all of
your own decisions.

Son: Yes I do. If I want your
opinion, I will ask.

The approach on the left opens the door to joint solution finding while the one on the right closes the door, damaging any trust that has been built up between the father and the son. As I write this, I acknowledge that I have been guilty once or twice of Scenario 2. As I reflect on it, I realize that my reaction is rooted in my belief system about what respectful communication with adults looks like. Regardless of the reason, the style in Scenario 2 closes the door to effective problem solving, while Scenario 1 encourages the child to voice their viewpoint and feel heard.

The guidelines listed here scratch the surface of the journey toward expressing emotion freely and tolerating free emotional expression among others—especially our children. Again, these things will take time before they become habits but if you are committed, embracing the emotional man you are is a critical step on your journey to becoming the great dad you never had. Our final lifelong lesson "Fill the Fatherhood Bag," is a short but powerful one. Keep going!

Chapter 12 - Lesson #7
Fill the Fatherhood Bag

If you have made it this far, it means one of two things. Either you have lots of time on your hands or you have found some nuggets in the information shared in the previous chapters. I am hoping you are here because of the latter reason. This is the final life lesson that I share in this book and it is one that has certainly served me well throughout my time as an adult. As a young aspiring military officer, I was totally intrigued by the various leadership styles utilized in the profession of arms. While sitting in a military science class, one of my professors described a metaphor for leadership development that I found to be simple but rather profound. His concept was the leadership bag. He mentioned that throughout our military career, we would encounter many different leaders. Some of them would be highly effective while some would continually make you question their competence and decision making. Some would demonstrate universal leadership strategies while some would provide fantastic insight into leadership approaches that were effective in specific situations.

"You will be exposed," the instructor stated, "to the strengths of many leaders. But you will also have close enough access to see some of their weaknesses and flaws on display. Some of the examples that you encounter will be beacons of positive leadership. Several will give insight into what not to do as a leader. Both are equally valuable and should be used to help shape you as a leader. As you encounter them, think of your imaginary leadership bag that is always slung over your shoulder. Take anything that impresses you from the leadership situations you encounter and throw it into your imaginary leadership bag. Your leadership bag will contain your lessons learned. At times in your career, when faced with new or complex leadership challenges, you will be able to dig into your leadership bag and draw relevant tidbits from your previous encounters."

As I thought about this symbol of the leadership bag, my analytic nature led me to think about some of its characteristics that made it such a great tool. First, the bag is always with you. You always have the opportunity to see a random display of leadership that you would like to record for future reference and could quickly do so by throwing it into "the bag." Second, its contents are varied. The leadership bag contains leadership nuggets from all kinds of leaders, many different leadership styles and with many different outcomes. Third, it is bottomless, meaning that it will never be too full to hold the next thing you would like to throw into it.

With this lesson embedded in my memory, I have gone through my entire professional career filling and digging into my leadership bag. It has forced me to be more observant of leaders in action, and to never hesitate to use it to find solutions to daily leadership challenges. Interestingly, as I mature, I also find myself discarding contents of my bag that I find are no longer relevant to the type of leader I wish to become. The fact that I can add items to and remove items from my bag gives me the ability to freely evolve, changing as I grow, and effectively mitigating the risks associated with the Conflict of Learned Behaviors that I described before. Additionally, my leadership bag allows me to operate like an amalgamation of many of my leadership heroes, borrowing from each of their strengths and learning from their mistakes as well.

So, how has this imaginary bag really helped me? I am glad you asked. I am now able to comprehend and utilize the political realms of leadership because of some great lessons in my bag from my mentor and Sacramento stalwart Scot Syphax. I understand aspects of servant leadership so much better now as a result of my interaction with my life coach Claudia Dias who has spent a 30+ year career serving the emotional needs of many of the underserved in Northern California. I have at my disposal examples that illustrate the leadership value of building powerful networks that I "stole" from my long-time friend and business partner Dr. Addie Ellis. Leadership behaviors that demonstrate humility, graciousness and empathy are all stuffed into my bag because of the years during which I had the luxury of watching my mother uplift and educate the communities in which we lived. I would venture to say that I am a stronger leader because I am a collage of the situational impacts these outstanding individuals have made on my life.

This metaphor of creating a leadership bag can be applied to any particular skill or competency you would like to develop over time. The pattern is simple. First, identify the capability you are trying to develop. Second, determine a base group of individuals within your circles who have that capability. Third, learn more about these individuals and follow closely the moves they make. Place in your "bag" the actions and skills you see them display that you would like to emulate. Finally, grow the network of individuals from whom you can select items for your bag.

Based on this pattern, it is clear that we can apply this to fatherhood. As a matter of fact, I can vouch for how this approach has really helped me over the years. Prior to becoming a dad, I started the process of constantly looking out for positive behaviors from dads I encountered and hoped to emulate someday. I watched on as I encountered coaches committed to being teachers for their daughters and sons, uncles who were dead set on being present despite less than perfect circumstances, workmates who recognized the importance of balance and dedicated their time and emotional vigilance to their families and friends who fought through significant adversity to tackle fatherhood head on. Additionally, the many strangers who I saw pushing strollers in the neighborhood or squealing with laughter as they swung, slid, crawled and jumped with their children in the parks were an inspiration. All of these people have unknowingly contributed to my personal fatherhood bag.

Interestingly, all seven of the lifelong lessons captured in this book are related to items that were stored in my fatherhood bag. Some of them were in my bag from a long time ago. Others were recently added. If I were to search through my bag, I am guaranteed to find numerous scenarios that remind me of how I should establish, document and live by a written contract with my children. I would also have several scenarios thrown in my bag that demonstrate how to build up my own resilient qualities and become a better model/teacher for my sons. There are also a few items that are reminders that I should calibrate my life with goals I have set for my own achievements and not goals that are in relation to the accomplishments of my father—being the best me and not a better him. The importance of my presence and how I show up for my sons as an emotionally intelligent and emotionally aware man are also illustrated through items that I have, on some occasion, thrown into my bag.

Now, I know you understand that this is a metaphor and you are never literally throwing items into a bag. So how will you actually throw items in your "fatherhood bag"? My recommendation is to start journaling. Create a special place where you can jot down experiences, ideas and inspirational events. Record the outstanding fatherhood acts you see and describe how you envision living them out with your children. Challenge yourself to put something in and pull something from your fatherhood bag for reuse on a daily basis. Surround yourself with "visual controls"—artifacts that remind you of the contents in your fatherhood bag. These artifacts may be pieces of art, photos, videos, quotes, sound clips that inspire you to achieve the greatness that you strive for as a father.

Chapter 13
Coming to Closure

So here we are nearing the end of our conversation. You stuck it all the way through and I am very impressed. My only desire is that I have encouraged you in some way. At a minimum, I hope I have helped you visualize the possibilities that lie before you as a father—whether you are already serving in that role or if you are a young aspiring dad. I have learned over time that, despite the commitment, time, energy and sacrifice required for you to effectively father your children, it is by far the most rewarding capacity in which you can serve. You may never win a Father of the Year award, or you just might. But regardless, you have the chance to be a hero in the eyes of your offspring.

Many of you who read this cover to cover and stayed with me on this journey may share my experience of having an apathetic father, no father presence at all, or maybe you had a taste of both. This experience, though important, does not have to be at the core of your identity. As in our discussion on resilience, it can be used as a motivational force that propels you to higher heights as a man, father and significant other.

Some of you may simply be indirectly affected by fatherlessness due to a close affiliation with a man who was fatherless. Maybe you are in a relationship with one, are married to one, or actually raised one. Maybe you are one to whom those with this experience turned to as a substitute. My goal in sharing this book with you was to move the idea of fatherlessness and its impacts on men from your blind spot and into your peripheral vision. As you interact, consider the lens through which these men have experienced their transition from childhood to adolescence to adulthood. Consider the unanswered questions that they probably still deal with up to today or will most likely develop with time.

The unanswered questions that persist stoked many conversations that usually ended up with a discussion on emotional closure. As we have established, there is an emotional element to the impact of fatherlessness. I believe that this element exists, regardless of where you fall on the continuum of actions that led to the fatherless experience. Whether you are fatherless as a result of apathetic fathering, abandonment or anything between the two, I think that ultimately they are questions that arise, particularly around identity and the completion of one's identity. It is for this very reason that most of the men I have interviewed or with whom I had conversations agreed that despite the important role many substitutes played, they simply fell short in providing emotional closure. While coaches, teachers, pastors, mentors and even stepfathers may have provided a guiding force, they could never answer the questions on identity completion.

One story stood out for me. One of the men I spoke to was in his early fifties and met his father for the first time when he was 41 years old. After two decades of failed attempts to connect with his father, he took it upon himself to locate and pay a surprise visit to his dad. As he shared his story with me, he recounted that prior to meeting his father, the pain of not even knowing him was haunting. He outlined the numerous questions he faced on a daily basis stating "My pain lived with me daily…I would think about what he looked like, what he sounded like, how he stood, how he walked. I would think about everything about him. I would literally look at strangers sometimes and wonder if that person was my father, and that was until I met him at the age of 41. It was just like I have to go find this guy. I can't live like this anymore. I need just to look at him."

Upon meeting his father, this man described the experience as surreal. He shared that he was speechless and experienced what felt like a scene from an animated movie. As he looked as his father, his focus zoomed in on physical traits—his father's height, hairline, eyebrows, eyes, gait, deep voice. He also quickly recognized many mannerisms in his father that he himself had. "Now I see why I walk like that! That is where I got this deep voice from! I also got my hairline from him, too!" These were his thoughts as he quickly processed through elements of his own identity completion.

As corroborated by many who have lived this and as this gentleman demonstrated, emotional closure after fatherlessness is highly important to one's wellbeing. This closure is different for every person. For some, it may come in the form of identity completion like the gentleman I mentioned before. For others, it could take the form of getting answers to the unanswered questions. Why? What circumstances led to this? How could you not think I needed you? And for some, it could take the form of unpacking the pain and frustration and getting to the point of forgiveness.

Despite the importance of closure, so many of us are driven by the feelings associated with abandonment or neglect, and carry anger, an inability to let go and dare I say hatred at our situations. All of the fatherless men with whom I conducted research indicated that going to the source of your pain was a start in the journey of emotional closure. Each of my mentors and coaches suggested that having a candid conversation with my father was something I should do. However, I was stubborn, stuck in my comfort zone of using my experience as fuel even though I knew following their advice was something I needed to do.

So, with that in mind, for fifteen years I attempted to approach my father to get his clarification and understand his side of the story. Each time I encountered him, I was blocked by my own recollection of incidents. On a few occasions I was thrust into anger because I could detect that he had relapsed and was drinking again. For fifteen years I attempted and fifteen years I failed.

A year ago, I visited again and decided I would give it a shot one more time. Upon visiting my father, I learned from family members that he recently started drinking again after almost three years of being sober. He was committed to a psychiatric hospital for evaluation after evidence that the prolonged alcohol consumption had taken its toll on his mental wellness. Reluctantly, I went to visit him at the hospital.

When I finally made it through the administrative red tape and connected with him, I was shocked at his physical degradation and his meekness. After the pleasantries, I asked him directly about the factors that led to his admittance into the hospital to which he candidly replied "It's the drinks!"

"But what about the people that are around you that are encouraging you to mess with *the drinks*," I shot back. I was not prepared for what would happen next. In a rather matter-of-fact manner, my father stated he knew what he needed to do but then began describing the type of funeral he wanted.

"I don't want a fancy casket, Dave" he said calmly. "I want a simple box, not a lot of people, just something quick!"

"TIME OUT!" I said while signaling frantically like a basketball coach in the last seconds of a close game. "We are not talking about your death but how you can ensure that you live longer."

Once I said that, everything slowed down to a crawl as I quickly processed my belief system about my father and about alcoholism in general. My father lost everything that mattered to him—a phenomenal wife in my mother, two sons filled with potential, and a way of life that he never recovered. I had always viewed alcoholism as a result of his actions, as a choice he made that deprioritized his family. It was poor decision making, selfishness and a refusal to confront his problem that led to his demise. But for the first time, I heard something different. I was taken back to that moment on my 30th birthday when the questions about my fatherless experience changed and how that change influenced the next decade of my life. At this moment, I finally realized that at the root of my frustration and hatred was my father's relationship with alcohol. I could hear the resignation in his voice as he described the funeral he wanted. He had given up. I synthesized this observation with all that he had lost and thought.

"There is no way someone would subject themselves to such a life on purpose. Could it be that alcoholism is really a disease? Could it be that it is not simply a negative choice rooted in selfishness and instant gratification?" These questions swirled as I got back into the moment after what seemed like an eternity in thought but was only a few seconds.

"You know," I said uncontrollably, "regardless of all that we have been through, and all of the negative feelings that I held onto, I want you to know that I forgive you and that I truly love you!" I must admit that I too was shocked at the words that came from me. That was the first time in my 40 years of living that those words were ever used in a conversation that included my father. He had a physical reaction to what I said. He let out one loud sigh. We hugged and I walked away without another word uttered. I was in tears as I walked back to my car.

In the days that followed, I felt like a burden was lifted from me. I realized that to live out my potential as a great dad, I had to release anything that bound me to my past. A decade removed from those questions I had asked on my 30th birthday, I have developed some clarity around it to know now that no, it wasn't my fault at six years old and in your situation, it wasn't yours either.

About The Author

Dr. David Inniss has had a lifelong intrigue with the state of fatherhood and fatherlessness in society. Having experienced fatherlessness, David views father absence and paternal apathy as a key social issue that weakens families, communities and cultures. He is a father, speaker, author, professor and management consultant. When David is not in the classroom enlightening college students or with his boys creating memories, he is working as the Founder and CEO of management consulting firm The Koci Group®, helping companies around the world maximize human productivity in their organizations. David holds a Bachelor's of Science in Computer Science from the United States Military Academy (WestPoint), a Master's in Business Administration from California State University Sacramento (CSUS) and a Doctor of Education with a concentration in Human Resource Development from Drexel University. Originally from the beautiful island of Barbados, David now resides in Sacramento, CA.

For more information or to contact David directly, please visit www.drinniss.com.